A War Made in Russia

A War Made in Russia

SERGEI MEDVEDEV

Translated by Stephen Dalziel

polity

Polity Press
65 Bridge Street
Cambridge CB2 1UR, UK

Polity Press
111 River Street
Hoboken, NJ 07030, USA

ISBN-13: 978-1-5095-5839-1- hardback
ISBN-13: 978-1-5095-5840-7- paperback

A catalogue record for this book is available from the British Library.

Library of Congress Control Number: 2022950231

Typeset in 11 on 14pt Warnock Pro
by Cheshire Typesetting Ltd, Cuddington, Cheshire
Printed and bound in Great Britain by TJ Books Ltd, Padstow, Cornwall

The publisher has used its best endeavours to ensure that the URLs for external websites referred to in this book are correct and active at the time of going to press. However, the publisher has no responsibility for the websites and can make no guarantee that a site will remain live or that the content is or will remain appropriate.

Every effort has been made to trace all copyright holders, but if any have been overlooked the publisher will be pleased to include any necessary credits in any subsequent reprint or edition.

For further information on Polity, visit our website:
politybooks.com

Contents

Part III The War Nation

Introduction:
Method in this Madness

1

My favourite subject in school was history. We were taught by Galina Rudolfovna. She was very strict, had a veritable beehive hairdo; wore glasses as thick as the bottom of a bottle and spoke in a dogmatic manner. She also happened to be the leader of the school's Communist Party cell. Marxist ideology was the white charger on which she rode, and in triumphant tones she expounded to us the indestructible logic of Marx's version of history. She explained its base and its superstructure; who the productive forces were, and their relationship to the means of production; and the changes in social and economic formations. I liked the harmony of this structure and the power with which it provided answers to every question. But the school course did not stop there. Galina Rudolfovna went further, telling us about the roots of Marxism and about classical German philosophy. She introduced us to Friedrich Schelling and Georg Hegel and explained the logic of his view of history. My teenage imagination was seized by the 'vicious mole of nature' metaphor drawn from *Hamlet* by Hegel: he wrote that the world spirit imperceptibly digs in the thickness of history and comes to the surface in the form of an ideal state. For the philosopher, this meant the modern Prussian kingdom, which continued the splendour of Frederick the Great. Hegel explored this further in his *Lectures on the Philosophy of History*, maintaining that when the mole goes on digging, we have to listen to it.

Sitting in the classroom, brightly lit by fluorescent lights, I would gaze out of the window at the late autumn dawn that was hazily breaking over Moscow. Grey buildings and bare trees stared back at me. I remember those last years of the Soviet Union as a dull, cold time. There were queues in the shops; patriotic songs playing on the radio; people spoke in half-whispers – the grown-ups talked about nuclear weapons, Academician Andrei Sakharov, the war in Afghanistan. Cemeteries in Moscow were filling up with rows of fresh graves of lads in paratrooper berets only a little older than I was – and my classmates and I understood that it was essential that we moved on to higher education so that we could defer military service. In November that year, 1982, Leonid Brezhnev died, and he was followed by a procession of different general secretaries. The Soviet Union entered a shadow world. The country died after a few more years, suddenly expiring, as often seems to happen to the state in Russia; it went out with a whimper, not a bang. But those school lessons on Hegel's philosophy stayed with me, as did the Shakespearean image of 'the mole of nature' and the desire to listen to its relentless digging and to search for the logic in historical events.

Forty years later, Russia is again waging a colonial war on the territory of a neighbour, Ukraine. Once again, patriotic songs are being heard, the rows of graves are lengthening, the fear of a nuclear strike has returned and people are talking in kitchens in half-whispers. People were expecting this war. British and American intelligence warned it was going to happen. Yet, even so, hardly anyone believed that in the twenty-first century a major state, a member of the UN Security Council, would up and invade a neighbouring country with large army units comprising some quarter of a million people, to try to seize its territory and depose the lawful government. It was as if we were still in the depths of the twentieth century; or, perhaps more accurately, the fifteenth or sixteenth centuries. Europe had seen nothing like this since 1945. If we look a little wider, we can remember only Saddam Hussein's invasion of Kuwait in August 1990. The war that Russia started in Ukraine in 2022 is a massive geopolitical rift and has signalled the collapse of the whole international security system. It is a tragedy for Ukraine, but also a disaster for Russia, which has been torn away from the global community, and now the country is in free fall.

No one can yet predict the scale of this collapse. We are tumbling downwards along with the avalanche, desperately trying to stay on top of it so that we do not get buried alive. There is a great temptation to put this down to the madness of one man, who stamped on the edge of a dangerous cliff and set off this avalanche; or to blame the Russian elite, who are mired in a swamp of resentment and an inferiority complex. We could just call it all 'Putin's war', or 'the post-empire syndrome', but that would be retreating from my objectivist view of history. To use another phrase from Shakespeare, this book is an attempt to find some 'method in this madness': to find some sort of legitimacy in this disaster; to fit it into the logic of Russian history, into the phases of the life and death of the Russian Empire, into the structures of Russian politics, society and the mass consciousness. In other words, it is an attempt to discover the objective nature of this war. This has been long prepared for, breaking through, rather like the mole, in the fullness of time, and bursting out as Putin's state unleashing the largest and bloodiest slaughter seen in Europe since the Second World War.

2

War has always been a way of life for the Russian state, its very *raison d'être*. The state arose at the dawn of the modern era on the eastern edge of Europe, 'squeezed between Lithuania and the Tatars', as aptly put by Marx. It had constant battles with the expanding empires of the West on one side, and with the horsemen of the Eurasian steppe on the other. Looking westwards, the state's principal task was predominantly one of defence: for centuries it had to beat back attacks by European armies. In the seventeenth century, there were the Poles and the Lithuanians; it was the Swedes in the eighteenth; Napoleon came in the nineteenth, followed by more French invaders and the British in Crimea; at the start of the twentieth century, Germany and Austria attacked, and then Hitler invaded in the middle of the century. All of this helped to form what the nineteenth-century Russian historian Vasily Klyuchevsky described as the 'combative order of the state' (*boyevoi stroi gosudarstva*), a state always geared for war. As far back as the eighteenth century, Russia was forced to create a defensive line that stretched for over 2,000 kilometres from the Black Sea to the Baltic. This was made up of a double line of forts, placed a day's march from each other; but this still failed to prevent further invasions. As a result of these wars, Russia was the only one of the early empires of the modern era that survived a clash with the West, while all of the others – the Mesoamerican empires of the Aztecs and the Incas, those of the Safavid Dynasty in Persia and the Great Moguls in India, the Qin Dynasty in China and the Tokugawa Shogunate in Japan – succumbed to the pressure of a superior civilization, and became colonies or protectorates of Western countries. The Harvard historian Marshall Poe has called this 'the Russian moment' in world history, and he puts it down specifically to the way the Russian state and society were organized along military lines.[1] At the same time, Russia managed to extend its influence westwards, encompassing Poland, Finland and Bessarabia.

In the south and the east as well, Russia had to defend itself ceaselessly in the early centuries of its existence. In the thirteenth century, the Mongols seized the lands of Rus' and turned them into part of the western province of the Empire of the Descendants of Genghis Khan, the Ulus of Jochi. Even after the collapse of the Golden Horde two centuries later, Muscovy continued to fight against its remnants for a long time. Crimean–Nogai slave raids on Rus' continued until the end of the eighteenth century. From earliest times, a defensive rampart was created and strengthened on the southern and eastern borders to guard against slave raids from the steppe. This was similar to the Great Wall of China but located on the other side of the Great Steppe and made of wood, which was the basic building material used by the forest-dwelling Russian people. In the middle of the sixteenth century, Ivan the Terrible captured Kazan, capital of the Khanate of that name, which was one of the main legacies of the Golden Horde and a rival to Moscow. Ivan's crossing of the River Volga in Kazan began the ceaseless expansion of Russia to the east and the south that continued for the next 400 years. During this unprecedented expansion (Richard Pipes calculated that, in the sixteenth and seventeenth centuries alone, Russian territory grew by 35,000 square kilometres each year, an area which is comparable to the size of the modern-day Netherlands), Russia seized the whole of Northern Eurasia and became the largest continental empire in history.[2]

Such an expansion of territory demanded that the state be structured in a particular way, as did the endless wars and expeditions, influencing its relationship with the population and how it was administered territorially. Alexander Etkind has described this phenomenon as 'internal colonization', under which the state colonized its own people within its own borders, simultaneously moving these borders as it carried out external colonization.[3] Relations between the state and the population in Russia were never based on civil or republican models, but on colonial and exploitative ones. People were regarded as natural resources for achieving the state's strategic goals. In many ways, the colonization of Siberia and the Far East was brought about by military and policing tools, indeed by penal methods, rather like the colonization of Australia by the British Empire. The state built fortresses and prisons in the conquered lands, populating these huge frozen territories with soldiers, exiles and convicts. As a result, the territory of Russia came to be regarded in many ways as the embodiment of repression and penitentiaries. For centuries, Siberia has been not just a frontier, but a metaphor for fear of the state, a place of exile. Complete generations of enemies of the state vanished in the frozen wastes of Siberia, as did whole peoples. The area became a place of exclusion, punishment and oblivion.

External wars and internal colonization determined a special role for violence in the relationship between the authorities and society, and between the state and the individual. The whole territory of Russia became one of surveillance and police control, with virtually no place for civil organization or local autonomy. The military–feudal structure that developed in Russia meant that the basic function of the landed gentry was a military one: the nobleman received land from the state in order to breed recruits for the army and to report for duty with weaponry, horses and all the accompanying baggage when the sovereign called. A militarized elite developed in the country. From birth, a nobleman was assigned to a particular regiment; it is only from the second half of the eighteenth century that the nobility had the opportunity to perform regular civil service. For a large part of the population war became a routine, everyday activity, and the risk of being killed helped to form the well-known Russian sense of fatalism, the habit of gambling with fate. Yury Lotman, who has researched Russian culture in the eighteenth and nineteenth centuries, has written about this, citing it as evidence of the Russian's passion for card games and duels, so richly depicted in classical Russian literature.[4]

This 'combative order of the state' described by Klyuchevsky led to the particular role of the special services and the secret police as the custodians of state violence. With few institutional checks and balances placed upon them, they were granted unhindered access to the supreme power and gained a disproportionate influence over state policy. In Stalin's USSR, this led to mass terror wielded by the state security services. In effect, the Soviet Union became a terrorist state institutionalizing the state's war against its own population, and the Empire's against the outside world. From a mere instrument of the state, violence turned into its prime function.

Mikhail Gorbachev tried to break this mould, by lessening the world's fear of Russia, allowing for the break-up of the Soviet Empire in Eastern Europe and the growth of national self-awareness in the republics of the USSR itself, and carrying out an unprecedented reduction in both Soviet nuclear and conventional strength. But his attempts were half-hearted, as were the subsequent reforms carried out by Boris Yeltsin. In dismantling the structures of imperial domination, they failed to touch the apparatus of internal violence, notably the KGB – or, as it has re-named itself in modern times, the FSB.[5] It has maintained its previous functions, its leverage and its way of thinking, and it has wormed its way organically into the new market structure of post-Soviet Russia as one of the main entrepreneurs of violence. What's more, the Chekists (as they like to call themselves, after the first Soviet secret police force, the Cheka) have retained the myth from Soviet times that they form a 'secret order', a hidden power that is ready to spring to the assistance of the state should there be a collapse of power.

. . . The year 1999 crept on. Russia had experienced a stormy decade of post-Communist transformation that had been labelled 'the wild nineties'. In 1998, the country had suffered a profound economic crisis. On 17 August, the government announced that it was defaulting on its short-term debt. By the end of the year, the rouble had tumbled to a third of its previous value, people's standard of living had fallen dramatically and the banking system was paralysed. Boris Yeltsin, who had survived a quintuple heart by-pass operation, effectively vanished from the scene and was spending long periods away from the Kremlin; his press secretary constantly used the euphemism that he was 'working with documents'. Having been scared by the default, Yeltsin's 'family' (that is, his daughter, his future son-in-law and his close circle of officials and oligarchs) were concerned about the transition of power and the guarantee of their own security, and were feverishly seeking his successor. Public opinion polls showed that the people were demanding stability, a strong state and a tough leader: a healthy, teetotal, middle-aged male – perhaps a general with combat experience or a representative of the special services, an intelligence officer. The figure who embodied that 'strongman' image demanded by the people and Yeltsin's entourage was the barely noticed executive director of the FSB, a colonel: one Vladimir Vladimirovich Putin. In August 1999, Yeltsin appointed him as acting head of the government of Russia and named him as his successor. The night of New Year's Eve 1999, as the millennium crept closer, Yeltsin announced his resignation, and Putin became acting president. In March 2000, he was elected president. A new century had begun in Russia – along with a new political era.

3

One of the key questions that this book is trying to answer is: is the war in Ukraine Putin's personal war, or is it all of Russia's war? Or, more broadly, is the present regime a random occurrence, created by one man, or the natural consequence of

Russia's long-term evolution? In their 2019 book, *Putin vs. the People: The Perilous Politics of a Divided Russia*, the political scientists Sam Greene and Graeme Robertson go for the second option: 'We need to think not of Putin's Russia, but of Russia's Putin. We need to understand that Putin is not above the country; he is of the country, of its politics, its society, and its history.'[6] Incidentally, almost twenty years ago, in 2005, the writer Viktor Pelevin, who is known for his aphorisms on contemporary Russian life, said that Russia had found its national idea: 'that's what Putin is'.[7]

The question about Putin is, first and foremost, a question about identity. In a time of multiple ruptures – the collapse of the Soviet Empire and of the socialist economy, the crisis of 'traditional values' and the onslaught of the global world – Russia was facing a deep identity crisis. The values of the Communist system had rotted and sunk into the past, and the global market had not proved to be a worthwhile replacement – and the 'Russian idea' was simply the pipe dream of some bearded freaks. Instead, Putin started to push the idea of nostalgia for Russia's great past and for the vanished lustre of the Empire.

Putin was not alone in this appeal to a former greatness; he even anticipated events in other parts of the planet. Trump came along with his message to 'Make America Great Again'; in Britain, Brexit reflected a nostalgia for the country being outside Europe; East European nationalists such as Viktor Orbán and Jarosław Kaczyński appeared, in Hungary and Poland respectively; and there was the rise of the ultra-right in Western Europe. Putin's turn towards conservative nationalism in many ways anticipated the rise of the authoritarianism of Recep Tayyip Erdoğan in Turkey; Narendra Modi in India; and Xi Jinping in China – and therefore we should not ignore the global appeal of Putinism. Nevertheless, his main message was for domestic consumption: rather like the hero of the cult films *Brat* [*Brother*] (1997) and *Brat-2* (2000), Danila Bagrov (the Russian equivalent of Rambo, who cured the USA of its 'Vietnam syndrome'), Putin promised to take revenge for the imagined 'insults done to Russia', and 'to raise Russia up off its knees'. The spin doctors who moulded Putin's image in 1999–2000 exactly caught the type that was needed: a strongman, terse and uncompromising, talking tough on terrorism without playing the liberal. Against the background of insipid politicians of the 'post-heroic era', Putin was shown to the world as the archetypal military chief: appearing now before the public in the cockpit of a jet fighter; next on the deck of a naval launch; then out horse-riding, baring his torso, thus creating one of the most memorable images of the past decades and throwing us back to an age of masculinity, patriarchy and naked power.

Putin has given back to Russia one of its main archetypes: war. He came to power as 'the war president' and has not left the subject alone even for a single year of his rule. His sudden appointment to the post of prime minister on 9 August 1999 coincided with the surprise attack on Dagestan by Chechen fighters two days earlier. Then there was a series of mysterious explosions in blocks of flats in Moscow, Volgodonsk and Buynaksk in the south of Russia in September 1999, which killed over 300 people and wounded a further 1,700. Another explosion was prevented in a block of flats in Ryazan, but this was then described as 'just an FSB exercise'. Chechen terrorists were blamed for the attacks, but there are theories that suggest that the FSB and Putin personally were behind the attacks, and that Putin wanted to raise his ratings as a protector of the nation ahead of the presidential election in 2000, as well as strengthening the role of the FSB and justifying a new war in Chechnya. One of those who strongly suggested that Putin played a role in this was the former FSB lieutenant-colonel, Alexander Litvinenko, who was poisoned with polonium by Russian agents in London in November 2006, according to an investigation by the British Special Branch.

Whoever was behind these explosions, the Second Chechen War sharply increased Putin's popularity, and his phrase 'We'll wipe out the terrorists in the shithouse' became a meme and the slogan of his first presidential term. This term was built on the global war against terror and coincided with the terrorist acts on 11 September 2001 in the USA and America's subsequent war in Iraq – which, at the time, Russia supported. However, this cooperation with the USA ended in September 2004, when Chechen terrorists seized a school in Beslan in North Ossetia. More than 300 children perished in the botched operation to free the hostages, but Putin unexpectedly blamed the attack not on Islamic extremists but on Western countries, who allegedly were standing behind the terrorists. From that point on, the focus of Putin's permanent war switched to the West. He blamed the West for the collapse of the USSR, which he described as 'the greatest geopolitical catastrophe of the twentieth century', and for subsequent attempts to weaken and dismember Russia.

By 2007, this ideology had been formulated into a particular sort of 'Putin doctrine', which he presented at the Munich Security Conference. He shocked his audience by launching into invective against the USA, the enlargement of NATO and the 'unipolar world', as well as by his announcement of Russia's sphere of interest, and effectively his declaration of a new cold war. Just one year later, in August 2008, Russia attacked Georgia, seizing a part of its territory, South Ossetia, and recognizing the independence of this quasi-state. According to the accounts of insiders, around this time the minds of the occupants of the Kremlin were gripped by a book by the Russian businessman and politician Mikhail Yuriev, called *The Third Empire: Russia As It Should Be*. It was a political fantasy, written as an alternative future history. As a result of global wars, by the middle of the twenty-first century an authoritarian Russia, led by Emperor Vladimir II, defeats the USA, and seizes the whole of Europe, Turkey and the Middle

East. The leadership may not have seen this book as a call to arms, but it was taken as the prophecy of an inevitable war with the West in the 2020s. The occupation of South Ossetia and Abkhazia, followed by the annexation of Crimea and a proxy war in Eastern Ukraine, merely convinced the Kremlin of the prophetic nature of the book.

To prepare for this future war, a massive rearmament programme was launched in Russia from 2011 to 2020, at a cost of 700 billion dollars. Alongside this, a plan for military reform was devised under the guidance of the civilian minister of defence, Anatoly Serdyukov, which was intended to enable the transition to a mobile, contract army. In 2013, the so-called 'Gerasimov Doctrine' was published, named after the chief of the General Staff of the Armed Forces, General Valery Gerasimov. This put forward the concept of 'hybrid warfare', which emphasized, together with military operations, non-military actions such as (among other things) political and diplomatic pressure, information wars, subversion and the removal of the leadership of an enemy country.

But the main change that has happened in Russia over the past fifteen years is that war has become the language of everyday life, just as militaristic rituals have become a part of state propaganda and daily routine. On one hand, the cult of the Second World War and the religion of 'the Victory' have been endlessly implanted into people's consciousness, and they have become the unofficial state ideology. On the other hand, militarism has crept into every aspect of life, in public celebrations and rock festivals, in schools and cinemas. Everywhere there have been exhibitions of military technology and small arms, children have been dressed up in army uniforms and have been taught how to assemble and strip down automatic rifles; even babies have been put in strollers that have been done up to look like tanks. In 2008, military parades began again in Russia, which had not happened since Soviet times, and each year since then ever heavier military vehicles have appeared on city streets, tearing up the asphalt and the city's infrastructure; even the ballistic nuclear missile, Topol-M, has been rolled out. Television presenters have positively drooled while talking about nuclear strikes on London and Washington, threatening to turn them into 'radioactive dust', and in his annual addresses to parliament Putin has shown animated films about Russian hypersonic nuclear missiles that can fly right around the globe. As far as the propaganda of war is concerned, Russia has turned into a North Korea of sorts.

War has captured the population's imagination; it has become attractive, even sexy. For two generations of Soviet people after the Second World War, the mantra was 'May there never be a war.' The Soviet state, led by people who had lived through that war, proclaimed the struggle for peace – in words, at least. But all this has changed in the twenty-first century, as people have been seduced by slogans of revenge, and Putin's promise 'to raise Russia up off its knees'. A frivolous sticker has appeared in the rear windows of millions of cars all over Russia. It shows the Soviet crest, the hammer and sickle, raping the fascist swastika. Under the picture is written the slogan: '1941–1945. We Can Repeat It'.

4

War was the main theme of my previous book published by Polity Press, *The Return of the Russian Leviathan*.[8] To be more precise, it told of four internal 'wars' that an increasingly authoritarian regime was waging during Putin's third presidential term, from 2012 to 2018, when he had returned to power following the brief, cowardly and, actually, fictional 'thaw' under Dmitry Medvedev (2008–12). That period ended with Russia's unsuccessful 'revolution of dignity' in the winter of 2011–12, marked by street protests by the urban populations of Moscow and other large cities. The authorities' response to this was to switch on the machinery of repression and political terror – and it has been operating ever since.

The first of the four wars I described in the book was 'The War for Space'. Like a classic state of centuries past, Russia had become obsessed by the idea of seizing territory, from the grandiose claims on the Arctic (that 1.2 million square kilometres of the waters of the Arctic Ocean, including the shelf that goes up to Canada, belong to Russia) to the annexation of Crimea and the occupation of regions of Eastern Ukraine in 2014; from the colonial war in Syria to the taking over of squares and boulevards in Moscow by police squads in order to clear out protesters.

The second was 'The War for Symbols': the signs of authority, of power and of the sacralized 'sovereignty' that became a fetish under Putin's rule. Strategic missiles became a particularly important symbol, featuring on T-shirts and advertising hoardings; television showed the bizarre Russian sport of the 'Tank Biathlon'; and right in the centre of Moscow a monument was erected to the creator of the Kalashnikov rifle, as if this were Russia's greatest contribution to world civilization.

The third war was 'The War for the Body', about the government's interference in the private lives of citizens, in their physicality, their sexuality and their eating habits; in the life of the family and reproductive policy: all covered by Michel Foucault's term 'biopolitics'.[9] The authorities introduced laws against LGBT people that are fascist in nature (something that unites all authoritarian regimes is a hatred of homosexuality); they forbade foreigners from adopting Russian orphans (the so-called 'Dima Yakovlev Law', which the people nicknamed 'the cannibals' law'); they introduced sanctions on the importing of Western foodstuffs and destroyed banned products, crushing them with bulldozers and burning them in mobile crematoria.

Finally, the fourth war was 'The War for Memory'. The state began actively to push a memorial policy, publishing new history textbooks that created a single myth about Russia's greatness; imprisoning those who preserved the memory of Stalin's terror (such as the historian Yury Dmitriev, from Karelia); implanting a state religion of the Victory in the Second World War, with its own cathedrals, pilgrimages and the cult of the dead. A militarized society was created in Russia, one that dreamt about the myths of the Second World War and was ready for confrontation with the outside world. But a genuine hot war still seemed far off and unthinkable.

Three years ago, when *The Return of the Russian Leviathan* was published, would it have been possible to foresee the war in Ukraine? Probably, yes. The warnings and the signs had been spread far and wide, but I admit that I did not realize the depths of this imperial transformation of Russia and the extent of the threat to the modern world. In the same way, right up to the last moment, until the morning of 24 February 2022, I did not believe that there could be a full-scale war between Russia and Ukraine. But on that most sinister of mornings, when the news came through about the bombardment of Kyiv and the start of the Russian invasion, I saw how the four wars that I had written about in my book had come together in one real war, the kind that my generation had seen only in the cinema: with peaceful towns being bombed, columns of tanks moving across Ukrainian fields, railway stations overcrowded with refugees clutching their bundles of belongings and their tearful children; with charred corpses, blood, pain, torture and mass executions. The whole bloody history of the twentieth century that we thought we had lived through and had buried rose up out of the ground and engulfed us in these terrifying months. War has gone from being a rhetorical figure and an analytical paradigm to being a daily reality, a black funnel that spins ever deeper and ever stronger – an apocalypse in which we are living, and to which there is no end in sight.

5

This book is an attempt to trace the roots of Russia's current war in Ukraine, to understand the reasons behind it, how it is linked to the logic of Russian history and the behaviours of Russian society and the way in which Russian politics operates. **Part I, 'The Anatomy of Violence', looks at the practice of violence**, which runs through the whole of Russian society, from the family and school to state institutions. In this sense, Russian society is archaic, based as it is on the traditional hierarchies of authority, power and subordination. We see this in the relationships between parents and children; teacher and pupil; boss and staff; husband and wife. Despite the modernization that happened in the USSR in the twentieth century and the post-Soviet emancipation of many areas of life, notably in the major cities, violence and subordination are still widespread.

A typical example of the horizontal violence in society is demonstrated by the patterns of traffic on Russian roads and highways. This is not simply about movement in a particular space, where everyone is equal before the law and the rules of the road, thus optimizing the flow of traffic and minimizing the risks – it is a constant affirmation of status, reproducing the complicated hierarchical system that depends on the make and value of your car, the size of its engine, your number-plates, whether you bear special signs; it is a constant battle for respect and a demonstration of your position in the pecking order, in the course of which the participants raise the stakes and maximize the risks – which is why there are so many minor accidents on Russian roads.

Violence, now normalized and legitimated, is spread thinly throughout Russian life. It is no coincidence that violence features time and again in Putin's populist pronouncements, thus granting it the highest sanction of the state and securing him the support of the majority of the population. Having begun his time as president with the call to 'wipe out the terrorists in the shithouse', he continually repeats this mantra, with phrases such as 'the weak get beaten' and by calling on people to 'be the first to strike'. Violence is the standard operating procedure for the institutions of power and of law and order: the police, the army, the prisons and the FSB. Alongside the many videos produced by Alexei Navalny about corruption in the higher echelons of power in the last decade in Putin's Russia, one of the most frequent revelations in social media has been the evidence of torture in Russian prisons, corrective colonies and police stations. Every few months, the public have been presented with shocking videos of prisoners being tortured by police, investigators or prison staff. Every time this happens, people call for an investigation and for the culprits to be punished; but, every time, the state has remained silent, restricting its actions to a formal reprimand or a transfer of those responsible to another place of work – and the conveyor belt of torture has ground on uninterrupted.

In the same way, police brutality has increased over the past ten years as they have broken up opposition meetings. Heads have been smashed, legs broken, demonstrators have been beaten, with no consideration given to their age or their sex, from 15-year-olds to 80-year-old grandmothers. This has not been prevented by the law; indeed, it has been supported and approved of by the authorities. There was the well-known call by Putin's press secretary, Dmitry Peskov, 'to smear the demonstrators' livers across the asphalt'; and the Head of Rosgvardiya,[10] Viktor Zolotov, threatened to beat to a pulp the Russian opposition leader, Navalny, turning him into 'a juicy chop'.

Over the past decade, from the 'Bolotnaya Affair' in 2012 (the repression of people who took part in the protest meetings on Bolotnaya Square in Moscow) to the invasion of Ukraine in 2022, in every sense the Russian state has been actively working on the body of the nation. This has meant not only a greater variety of tortures and police violence, but the declaration of the state's absolute control over the physical body of the citizen. As mentioned above, in recent years a part of the authoritarian turn in Russia has been the biopolitics of power: the state has begun to regulate and control physicality, carrying out an active demographic, hygiene and sanitary policy, interfering in questions of sexuality, the upbringing of children, diet and personal hygiene. As far as the state is concerned, the population has become just another strategic resource ('the new oil', in the ironic Russian expression), not because people are seen as human capital, but because they are regarded as an attribute of the great state and a reserve for the armed forces. Putin has spoken on more than one occasion about it being his dream to have a population of 500 million people in Russia; at present, it is around 140 million.

An important episode in Russia's 'politics of the body', and one that helped to prepare the way for the war in Ukraine, was the Covid pandemic, the most serious phase of which occurred in 2020–1. The Russian authorities lost the battle with the pandemic. Despite the existence of an elaborate system for defence against an epidemic (a legacy of Soviet times), and even though Russia was one of the first countries in the world to come up with an effective vaccine, Sputnik-V, they were unable to organize the vaccination programme quickly enough, or to provide suitable medical help outside Moscow. As a result, Russia registered one of the highest excess death rates in the world (more than a million in 2020–1). Unlike the developed countries, the Russian government and regional authorities failed to provide the population with any significant material support, which effectively made quarantine and lockdowns futile, and at the same time brought down the private sector of the economy. The state's indifference to the health of the population was reflected in people's indifference to their own health and safety: the levels of Covid denial and the size of the anti-vaccination movement in Russia were among the biggest in the world. Covid taught the Russian authorities a vital lesson: when there is total lack of trust among the population, atomization of society and a failure of institutions, you can ignore the population and just hold on to the illusion of 'normalcy' and 'social stability' – the people are submissive, inert, fatalistic and prepared for any sacrifices.

At the same time, the pandemic brought about a permanent 'state of emergency' in the country, and the 'war against the virus' taught people to make a daily count of the victims. Using the pretence of 'infection control', active street protests were completely banned, including even single-person pickets. New ways were introduced to falsify voting in elections (hold them early, vote from home, let local officials create their own polling stations – what became known as 'voting on tree-stumps'). President Putin shut himself away in his bunker for many months, isolated from both the country and his closest advisers. Anyone who came near him had to spend two weeks in quarantine beforehand. It may well be that this confinement in the bunker led to him losing touch with reality even more and helped to push him to the decision to start the war.

This 'body turn' in Russian politics, examined in the first part of this book, went a long way to preparing the war in Ukraine. Politics came into the realm of physiology and biology, and was put at the limits of 'bare life', in the words of Italian philosopher Giorgio Agamben – be it in the acts of torture in prisons, the brutal breaking up of demonstrations, or in Covid hospitals. It's worth recalling here, too, the attempt to poison Alexei Navalny in August 2020 and his desperate fight for life. Violence, death and a warlike situation became the norm for life in Russia, an everyday occurrence. It was in these circumstances that Russia unleashed a war in February 2022: a war that, for its level of cruelty, for the numbers of civilian deaths and refugees, for the instances of genocide and annihilation of the Ukrainian people (mass rape of Ukrainian women, the filtration of Ukrainians through Russian camps, the exporting and forced adoption of Ukrainian children), has been unprecedented in post-Soviet history. But, in reality, this cruelty has been simply the projection and enlargement of the 'politics of the body' that has been carried out for a long time in Russia itself.

6

The second crucial element of this war is **memory – nostalgia and the historical policy** that the Russian authorities are actively pursuing. These are the issues covered in **Part II** of the book, '**The Memory Crusade**'. There are many aspects to the policy of memory, from the creation of a space for nostalgia for the Empire – such as the Zaryadye Park under the Kremlin walls – to the destruction of alternative projects for memory, ones that bring up some of the awkward questions from the past, such as the 'Memorial' society. The main element, though, is to support the myth about the Great Victory of 1945, which has become the state ideology.

In the past ten years, the policy of memory has become a mechanism for building an authoritarian regime in Russia and an instrument of its foreign policy. And Putin himself has become an amateur historian, regularly writing lengthy and pretentious essays about the Second World War. State propaganda has been able to play on Soviet nostalgia and post-imperial resentment to create a complete narrative of the history of Russia, emphasizing military victories and justifying Russia's past crimes, such as the Molotov–Ribbentrop Pact of 1939; the assassination of the Polish officers and intelligentsia at Katyn in 1940; the invasions of Hungary in 1956 and Czechoslovakia in 1968; or the colonial war in Afghanistan from 1979 to 1989. All these actions have now been rehabilitated and are described as having been in the interests of the state. The historical memory of Russia has been taken over by the state and used to legitimize the ruling regime, even to the point of inserting a new article in the latest edition of the Constitution of the Russian Federation in 2020, Article 67.1, which states that 'the Russian Federation defends the 'historical truth', although it is not clear what is understood by this 'truth'.

Putinism, in fact, is a sort of retro-politics. Having failed with his initial plans to modernize Russia and pursue a policy of rapprochement with the West in the period from 2000 to 2003, Putin started to turn to the past as the source of his legitimacy, as a force for the mobilization and consolidation of the population. Zygmunt Bauman calls such a policy 'retrotopia',[11] and Svetlana Boym writes about the 'epidemics of nostalgia' that construct an imaginary past and turn it into a political myth.[12] In general, this coincides with the global 'fashion for memory', the 'memorial era' as described by the French historian Pierre Nora: when they come up against the world of risk, uncertainty and the collapse of traditional institutions, nations turn to the past as the only reliable pillar of identity.

In the Russian case, the past is focused on the Second World War and the Victory of 1945, which have become the fundamental myth and a new religion for the nation. There is a place in it for the cult of the ancestors – people regularly hold pilgrimages under the name of 'the eternal regiment', at which they carry portraits of Second World War heroes in place of icons; they turn to them in difficult times and study their biographies. In the 'Patriot' military park just outside Moscow, a whole cathedral has been built, with a dome that has a diameter of 19.45 metres, in honour of the year 1945, and the steps of the porch are cast from German trophy weapons. On Victory Day in the park, a small copy of the German Reichstag is built out of plywood, and stormed by reenactors in historic military uniforms. The cult of Victory has seen the emergence of a popular movement ironically called 'Victory Frenzy': parents dress their children in wartime tunics, do up their strollers and bicycles to resemble toy tanks, teach them to sing military songs and make them look like Red Army soldiers.

In this sense, Russia's war in Ukraine is nothing more than a gigantic historical reconstruction. It is fitting that in its first stage, the seizure of the Donbas in 2014–15, the separatists were led by a well-known reenactor, Igor Girkin (pseudonym 'Strelkov'), who even used Stalin's orders from 1941 to execute people. In 2022, the historical reconstruction went even further. Russia created a cosplay of the Great Patriotic War: the initial idea of the war was absurdly announced as 'the denazification of Ukraine', in which Russia played the role of the Soviet Union at the time of the Second World War, and Ukraine was given the role of fascist Germany; the symbolic 'war of memory' was turned into a real, kinetic, war. And it was no coincidence that the head of the Russian delegation to the peace talks that took place in the early weeks of the war was the former minister of culture, Vladimir Medinsky, who is known for his apologist works on historical memory and 'myths about Russia'. Without this historical policy, nostalgia for the Empire and the myth of 'the Victory', this war would not have happened.

<h1 style="text-align:center">7</h1>

Finally, the third feature of this war is the way in which it has been **normalized** by Russian society and the elite, its acceptance as something natural – and that is what **Part III** of this book, **'The War Nation'**, is about. For many people, the greatest revelation of 2022 was not the actual attack on Ukraine on 24 February – which had often been predicted, expected and prepared for over the course of many years – but the reaction of Russian society, which accepted it as something perfectly normal. In March and April 2022, there was an expectation that the failure of the blitzkrieg and Russia's first military defeats, the wave of Western sanctions and the collapse of the rouble, the horrors of the war itself and the first casualties, would all open Russians' eyes to what was happening, lead to the dissatisfaction of the elite and, if not to unrest, then at least to social and political instability. But this did not happen. During the long holidays in early May, Russians went off to their dachas as usual, stoked up the barbecue, celebrated Victory Day on 9 May with their usual fireworks – then went home and carried on living normally, as if nothing was happening. The rouble grew stronger; the treasury's coffers took in the excess profits from the export of hydrocarbons, the price of which was rising (the simple arithmetic was that Russia was spending half a billion dollars a day on the war, while bringing in a billion in exports); sanctions turned out to be not as tough as feared; and the bulk of the population carried on living as before. They went to work, they raised their children and enjoyed life, apparently unaware that their country was destroying Ukrainian cities, killing, torturing and raping thousands of people, and turning millions into refugees. The journalist Masha Gessen found a striking image for this: they were like passengers flying in a modern airliner that, all the while, was bombing the cities beneath it.[13]

This illustrates a radically new condition of post-Soviet society that has come about over the course of Putin's two decades in power, with its anti-Western propaganda, militarism, repression and the destruction of political and civil institutions. At the same time, we cannot call this society 'totalitarian', because it is lacking an ideological mobilization. It is more accurate to talk about three different levels: the demobilization of society, the mobilization of the elite, and the legitimization of power. On the one hand, society has gone into a state of suspended animation and willingly uses the propaganda clichés about how Russia is not waging a war but a 'special operation', and how Ukraine has been taken over by 'Nazis' who are killing their own population. However absurd this picture is, it gives ordinary people psychological comfort. It does not contradict the version of events they're being fed and allows them to carry on with their everyday lives. Were they to step outside this myth, their whole worldview would collapse, something that people are too scared to contemplate. For centuries, Russians have been taught conformity by an evil and jealous state, something that has only grown stronger in Putin's time, when the authorities have found effective means to encourage loyal behaviour and repress dissent. Protest in society has been diffused and lost its voice, and where local examples burst out (as in the ever more rare demonstrations and mass actions, local election campaigns, social media and opposition media), the authorities employ targeted, concentrated repression, disciplining the population to the extent that in Russia today people are afraid even to say the very word 'war'.

On the other hand, managers who are embedded in the distribution chains of the state system (by the 2020s, two-thirds of the economy was state-run) enthusiastically follow the rules of mobilization: heads of schools and other state establishments, university rectors, chief hospital doctors and theatre directors draw up their staff in support lines, collect money for the front, and display pro-war propaganda on their walls and facades. Just like in the army, ordinary people follow the orders of the authorities. The higher echelons of the elite are also actively responding to the new challenges of import substitution, adapting to sanctions and running a wartime economy. At the summit of society, for the 'golden thousand' of the Russian elite, personal loyalty is a matter of life and death, inspired by fear of punishment should they voice any doubts or criticism. Any attempt to jump ship is seen as treason. As an example, there is the case of Anatoly Chubais: the former deputy prime minister in Boris Yeltsin's government, and director of major state corporations under Putin, left Russia and was hospitalized in Italy with a rare neurological condition in August 2022; he may well have been poisoned.

Finally, despite alarmist predictions at the very start of the war, the authorities have merely strengthened their legitimacy and have received a mandate for the continuation of military actions from the elite and a large proportion of the population. Despite clear distortions in opinion polls taken during the war, we can say that the majority of Russians either directly support this war, or regard it as inevitable, or – more than anything – simply ignore it, pushing it beyond the boundaries of their own perception. A unique wartime consensus has set in in Russia: with the voices of any objectors now silenced, the war in Ukraine has become a platform for consolidation for both the population and the authorities. As the director of the Hermitage Museum, Mikhail Piotrovsky, said in a scandalous interview in June 2022, 'On the one hand, war is blood and killing. But on the other hand, it's the people's self-affirmation, the self-affirmation of the nation.'

In this sense, the war with Ukraine gives a new definition to the Russian national idea, which the country has been seeking for thirty years, wandering in the desert of the post-Soviet transition, and ultimately finding it in this perverted form. Through this war, Putin's Russia has discovered its final shape. The 'state of emergency' that Putin has been constructing throughout his whole time in power has been reified in this 'special military operation'. In fact, Putin's whole time in office, from explosions at the apartment blocks in 1999, through the Sochi Winter Olympics, the annexation of Crimea and the amendment to the Constitution in 2020, has been one endless 'special operation', and now it has spilled beyond the borders of Russia.

8

And here we have the greatest danger: Russia has become the world's main exporter of war. In retrospect, this seems to have been Putin's strategic goal all along. If the late Mikhail

Gorbachev succeeded in neutralizing the Soviet threat and received 'the peace dividend', Putin has revived 'the Russian threat' and is seeking the war dividend. He believes that, playing from a position of weakness, Russia should endlessly raise the risks for all those around it. He spoke about this openly at the end of 2021, on the eve of the invasion, when he declared that 'a certain tension' had arisen in the West as a result of Russia's actions, and that the aim of Russian policy was to ensure 'that this situation remains so for as long as possible'.[14] The Kremlin's former chief ideologist, Vladislav Surkov, then developed the thoughts of his patron in an article entitled, 'Where Has Chaos Gone? Unpacking Instability', in which he maintained that Russia should become 'an exporter of chaos' to the outside world; the entropy that has built up in Russia should be exported 'for use on a foreign territory'.[15]

These declarations are evidence of strategic weakness. As it is unable to guarantee peace and stability, 21st-century Russia has begun to specialize in the production of risk as a way of promoting its interests, raising its global status and intimidating prospective rivals. By 2020, Russia had ultimately lost its economic and its diplomatic might and, as the first months of the war with Ukraine showed, its military power, too – as well as any attractiveness of its social model, its scientific and innovative potential, its achievements in Space, and, after the doping scandal in Sochi, its sporting prowess. The only elements of Russia's 'soft power' that remained were fear and the ability to spread tension. Over the course of the last twenty years, this has been shown by the perpetuation of conflicts and the creation of 'an anti-sanitary cordon' of toxic territories on the southern and western perimeters of Russia.

But in February 2022, this strategy of provoking conflict spilled over into an open war. What is more, in just the first few weeks, this war escalated from a regional conflict into an all-European one, with Russian threats towards Moldova and the Baltic States, with applications from Finland and Sweden to join NATO; and into a global one, considering the flows of Ukrainian refugees, Western sanctions against Russia, America providing weaponry to Ukraine, and the influence of the war on global markets for energy and foodstuffs. The globalization of Russia has finally taken place, but only in one capacity – as a global problem and as a source of war.

9

'Politics of the body', the cult of the dead and the cult of war are three classic components of fascism. One could add the cult of the state, the deification of the leader, the ideology of revanchism, as well as rabid anti-liberal and anti-Western rhetoric. As the Yale University historian Timothy Snyder noted, in his much-discussed article 'We Should Say It: Russia Is Fascist', 'People disagree, often vehemently, over what constitutes fascism. But today's Russia meets most of the criteria that scholars tend to apply.'[16]

Indeed, from the very start of the war that Russia announced as a crusade for the 'denazification of Ukraine', Russia itself showed signs of fascism, from the home-grown semi-swastika, the letter 'Z' – which was used to mark Russian military technology employed in the invasion and that has become a symbol of the new regime, displayed on T-shirts, posters and the facades of buildings – to the idea of the 'bonds' (*skrepy*), the gathering of traditional values that exactly matches the Italian word, *il fascio*, the ancient Roman lictor's bundle, the fasces: a rod with an axe, tied up with a ribbon, from which we derive the word 'fascism'. The sight of Russian armoured columns traversing the fields of Ukraine, setting fire to towns and killing civilians is a flashback to wartime footage of 1941–3, when Wehrmacht tanks trampled Ukraine in exactly the same way.

Furthermore, the striking examples of the genocide of the Ukrainian nation that Russia has initiated in the course of this war – killing by ethnicity; mass rape of Ukrainian women; strip-searching people in filtration camps to inspect their bodies to see what tattoos they have; the deportation of Ukrainian families for forced labour in Russia; and taking Ukrainian children for them to be adopted by Russian families – are all very reminiscent of the way in which Jews and 'lower races' were treated by the Third Reich. This prompted the London-based political scientist Vladimir Pastukhov to suggest that Russian fascism has evolved from the Italian corporate fascism to the German Nazism.[17] This idea is supported by articles in Russian state media, such as, for example, the Nazi manifesto of the political consultant Timofei Sergeitsev, published on the website of the government information agency RIA in April 2022, in which he calls for the total eradication of Ukrainian culture and identity: the 'de-Ukrainization' of Ukraine.[18]

However, despite all this, one key element of fascism is missing from its Russian breed: the ability to mobilize society. Yes, heads of schools line up their pupils in the form of the letter 'Z' for a grand display; bus drivers put stickers with the same letter on their vehicles, as instructed by their bosses; and deputies of the State Duma, TV propagandists and the former president, Dmitry Medvedev, every day come out with classic fascist rhetoric. Especially memorable was the leader of the Liberal Democratic Party of Russia, Leonid Slutsky, at the funeral of the propagandist Darya Dugina, in August 2022, chanting the slogan, 'One country, one president, one victory', which reminded many of the classic *Ein Reich, ein Volk, ein Führer*. But, for all this, the mobilization which started in Russia in September 2022 faces great difficulties and remains increasingly unpopular with the people. Those liable for mobilization are fetched from their homes and offices, sometimes from schools and kindergartens where fathers come to pick up their children. Private military companies, like the infamous 'Wagner', are recruiting new contract soldiers from prisons, with the promise of amnesty for their sentences after six months; from the homeless; and from the dregs of society. And in the so-called 'people's republics' of Donetsk and Luhansk, which have been occupied by Russia since 2014, men of service age are simply picked up on the streets and forcibly put in territorial defence units.

The problem is that the classic fascism of the twentieth century was a product of a mass industrialized society, while Putinism has come out of a post-Soviet, post-industrial and post-mass society, based on demobilization and atomization. The depoliticization of the population and the inability to carry out collective action is one of the main results of the twenty years of Putin's rule. This is a society built according to the laws of show and performance, and its principal instinct is for stability and comfort, not a burning desire or 'passionarity' (as the Russian ethnographer Lev Gumilev called it). Fascist symbols and slogans are left hanging in the air. The bulk of the population are prepared to support the war symbolically or in a declaratory manner, but they are not ready to go and die for the sake of Russia's imperial greatness.

Thus, Putin's version of fascism needs a qualifying prefix. The American philosopher Mikhail Epshtein proposed calling it *schizo-fascism*: 'fascism behind the mask of a battle against fascism', as if it were a split view of the world; in its own way, a caricature of fascism – albeit a dangerous and aggressive caricature.[19] It could also be called *cargo-fascism*, equating it to a 'cargo cult': indigenous tribes have been known to take as a symbol something from outside their tribe and worship it, giving it supposedly special powers. Over many centuries of interaction with the West and 'catching-up modernization', Russia managed to copy Western institutions and sociopolitical formats. In this case, Russia is reproducing the aesthetics of a twentieth-century totalitarian regime, all the while dreaming about the typical German *Ordnung* ['order in society'], efficiency and discipline.

Paradoxically, amidst all the rhetoric about 'the battle against fascism', Russia has its own particular nostalgia for fascism, linked to the cult television serial of the 1970s, 'Seventeen Moments of Spring'. It tells the story of a fictitious Soviet spy, Colonel Isayev, who is working in fascist Germany under the pseudonym of Max Otto von Stierlitz, a *Standartenführer* in the SS. Cleverly filmed in studio settings, this spy film seems to have been like ideological sabotage in the bowels of the Soviet consciousness, portraying Nazis as real people, and the SS *Standartenführer*, played by the cult actor Vyacheslav Tikhonov, became a heartthrob for Soviet women for many years. This image of the mysterious spy was burnt into the mass consciousness, and when people were searching for a new strongman as a leader after the crises of the nineties and the default of 1998, Vladimir Putin ideally fitted the bill as a decisive man of few words: a Stierlitz from the KGB. It is no coincidence that in 2022, as the war raged in Ukraine, a statue of Stierlitz was unveiled in front of the headquarters of the Foreign Intelligence Service (SVR) in Moscow – a statue of the ideal Soviet man, who happened also to be an officer in the SS.

This similarity between Soviet totalitarianism and Hitler's (making such a comparison publicly in contemporary Russia would lead to a prison sentence) allows us to give one more definition to the current Russian regime. It is retro-fascism, in the same way that Putinism is retro-politics, based on images from the past. But by resurrecting Stalinism and the terrorist practices of the NKVD (as the secret police were known for much of Stalin's time), Putin has simultaneously resurrected fascism, as this war clearly demonstrates. This raises a fundamental problem of history: the fact that the Second World War never really ended. In the 1930s and 1940s, the allied Western democracies were faced with two guises of totalitarian evil that were trying to take over the world – Hitler's Third Reich and Stalin's USSR. But only one was defeated in 1945, while the second one temporarily allied with the West, prevailed and transformed, and seventy-seven years later it has resurrected the guise of fascism that once again wants to reshape the world according to its own rules. In this sense, the war in Ukraine is simply a continuation of the unfinished Second World War.

10

Schizo-fascism, cargo-fascism, retro-fascism – no matter what we call Putin's regime, any comparison is lame, and it is simply a childish game to call your opponent 'a fascist'. We would be better off acknowledging the unique nature of this apparition. It is secondary and imitative in relation to the historic forms of fascism, but at the same time it is unmistakably Russian. From the very first days of the war, the derogative nickname 'Russism' was coined: a home-grown version of fascism, in which the cult of the state, post-imperial resentment, the centuries-old habit of violence and the aggressive policy of memory, and the cult of the dead, all come together. This regime and this war are a product of the decaying Russian Modernity: the unitary police state, a colonial economy, a paternalistic society, great-power chauvinism and militarism have all taken root. The war testifies to how archaic the country is, to its failure to modernize over the past thirty years, and to its final defeat in the encounter with the twenty-first century. It is this historic defeat of the Russian state project that has given rise to envy, resentment, the dream of revenge on modern civilization (an idea that goes back to Dostoevsky's 'underground man'), and the 'special path' of Russian culture – the whole complicated psychiatric pathology that lies at the base of Putinism, 'Russism' and the war in Ukraine.

Make no mistake, this is not a war for the 'imperial legacy', nor is it a regional conflict on the edge of Eastern Europe, as were Russia's earlier wars in Transdniestria, Abkhazia and South Ossetia. This is a world war, unleashed by Russia to overturn the modern liberal world order. It has many open and hidden global supporters, and there are neutral countries that are watching carefully to see how this challenge that has been thrown down to mankind pans out. The war in Ukraine is merely the prelude, and it does not matter whether Putin's regime triumphs (whatever he might call 'a victory') or he has to back down, he will continue to try to break the modern world, by using either 'hybrid wars' or open aggression, information sabotage or nuclear blackmail, until he suffers a decisive military defeat and the regime is utterly destroyed. What we have come up against here is not a temporary aberration, not the madness of a dictator who has overplayed his hand – nor is it simply the nostalgia of the older generation of Russians; it is a tectonic geopolitical process in the protracted decay of a huge Eurasian empire. The mole of Russian history has been digging away for thirty years through the thickness of the post-Soviet transition, and it has burst out onto the surface in the form of a bloody, archaic and pointless war: a war made in Russia.

PART I

THE ANATOMY OF VIOLENCE

The State Came after the Body

If you look at the themes and topics of the Russian media over the past few years, you cannot escape the images of the human body being subjected to violence – and frequently in the most graphic anatomic detail. One image is in a video that was obtained by the newspaper *Novaya gazeta*, in which the body of an inmate of the Yaroslavl corrective colony Yevgeny Makarov is shown spread out on a table in the 'education room'. He's howling and begging for mercy, while eighteen people are systematically beating him with truncheons, all the while commenting on how his legs are swelling up.[1] Another is an online photograph of the Ukrainian film director Oleg Sentsov on hunger strike in a prison hospital in the Arctic town of Labytnangi, with daily reports about the state of his health, his haemoglobin levels and his pulse.[2] Yet another image showed under-age schoolchildren in a cage in the court-room during the trial of the so-called 'New Greatness' case, where 17-year-old Anna Pavlikova spoke about being tortured during the investigation, and ending up with inflammation of her ovaries after lying on the cold floor of the interrogation cell.[3] These images could have come out of a book on the history of the Middle Ages; or perhaps from the classic work by

Michel Foucault, *Discipline and Punish*, in which he examines the history of technologies of violence and coercion in the modern age, starting with a vivid account of torture in the seventeenth century.

Torture has always played a role in the Russian machinery of repression. It is rooted in the traditions of the NKVD and the Gulag, and with every year its presence increases in our daily lives. According to witnesses, though, it did ease off somewhat from the 1960s through to the 1980s, following demands to observe 'socialist legality'. But after the chaos in law and order in the nineties and the start of the era of the *siloviki* (those from the so-called 'institutions of power' – the military, the Interior Ministry and the secret police) this century, torture has once again become a part of the repertoire of the police, the FSB and the prison service, the FSIN.[4] And in the past decade, as the system of law and order has grown larger and effectively become self-serving, new threats and criminal cases have been thought up, and these services have received increased budgets – and torture has become an essential element of the way the machine functions. It preys on the only resource it has available to it: the human body, squeezing the maximum use out of it, by confessions, discipline and slave labour. Recently, though, the revolution in smartphones and messaging systems has led to a critical mass of video evidence going viral on social media, and the problem has been exposed.

Still, despite an instant reaction from the FSIN and exemplary punishments of both the offenders and their bosses, the way the Makarov case was dealt with seemed to have the opposite effect to that intended. Nearly everyone was convinced that torture would continue just as severely as before, but with less publicity. The conclusions drawn were that members of the prison service would probably have their smartphones removed from them when on duty and they would be forbidden from using social media. Also, recordings made by surveillance cameras would be drastically edited. Millions of people all over the country watched the torture video from Yaroslavl, but beyond the public outrage that was voiced about it, it did not lead to any serious change. There was no significant social movement, no flash-mobs, no protests. We just understood that, alongside us, on the other side of a wall that is only an arm's length away, we have our very own Gestapo, a torture hell – one wrong move and you could end up there. Paradoxically, this video merely exposed what was already an open secret, and in the public consciousness torture became normalized and routinized. We carry on living, knowing that, should we happen to fall into the hands of law enforcement, either as a witness or as a defendant, in the police station round the corner they can string us up like a bird, make us sit on a bottle or put a bag over our heads.[5] And, according to a poll conducted by the sociological organization the Levada Centre, 7 per cent of respondents consider that 'prisoners have no right to expect to be treated normally', and a further 28 per cent hold that 'in certain circumstances it will be essential to use force on prisoners'.[6]

People in Cages

In the same way, we have grown used to the sight of people in cages in courtrooms. All the most well-known prisoners, from the former minister of the economy Alexei Ulyukaev to the theatre director Kirill Serebrennikov, have appeared on our screens in cages, like wild animals or particularly dangerous criminals – or like the famous rebel Yemelyan Pugachov, who led an uprising in the eighteenth century and before his execution was paraded through the streets of Moscow in a cage. Sometimes, instead of a cage there is a glass 'aquarium', but this seems to be even closer to Michel Foucault's idea of the 'panopticon' as a means of state control: the accused's body is on display like an exhibit in the Kunstkamera, exposed to the all-seeing eye. It is not surprising that the 'cages' and the 'aquariums' were the subjects of some of the most constant criticism of Russia in the Council of Europe when Russia was still a member.

Another recent video comes from Komsomolsk-on-Amur in the Russian Far East and shows a female schoolteacher beating an annoying second-year pupil – an 8-year-old. This is part of the same disciplinary norm. As Foucault teaches, in the society of the modern age, school is yet another institution for control, in the same way that prison is. And if the Moscow riot police, the OMON,[7] can drag schoolchildren face-down across the asphalt, as they did when breaking up young people's demonstrations in the spring and summer of 2017, then why can't a schoolteacher, another representative of the authorities, use similar measures against an obstinate child? Or threaten schoolchildren with the police, Putin's bodyguards and execution, for writing on the blackboard, 'Putin's a thief', as happened in the Siberian village of Tayezhnoye? A typical phrase used by the schoolteacher as she was beating the 8-year-old was, 'Who do you think you are?' And, indeed, who is he from the point of view of the state, when the state's disciplinary machine works to de-individualize the citizen and crush their will by directly using physical violence on their body?

An important shift in relations between the state and the citizen is taking place before our very eyes – at various levels, the authorities are ever more openly carrying out assaults upon people's bodies, thus violating Article 21, Paragraph 2, of the Constitution of the Russian Federation: 'No one shall be subject to torture, violence or other severe or humiliating treatment or punishment.'[8] The crusade for sovereignty and the archaic regression of the authorities have led to the state, like Hobbes's Leviathan, returning to its source code – applying violence to the body, by way of torture, imprisonment and degradation. Now that Russia has been expelled from the Council of Europe, the next logical step should be the return of the death penalty; abolition of the ultimate punishment was a condition of membership of the Council. From using modern ways of dealing with the collective body of the nation ('biopolitics'), the Russian authorities are returning to more archaic methods of legitimization, 'anatomopolitics' (torture) and 'thanatopolitics' (killing), in the terms of Giorgio Agamben.

The way in which Oleg Sentsov was dealt with serves as an example of a medieval relationship to the body of the individual. In his own words, after the annexation of Crimea, the Ukrainian film director was 'transferred along with the land' like a serf, forcibly converted to Russian citizenship and convicted on this basis under the laws of the Russian Federation. So violence was committed against Sentsov's body in three ways: firstly, he was arrested unlawfully; then he was tortured (he was beaten, suffocated with a bag over his head, and threatened with rape and murder, as described by Sentsov's lawyer in his application to the European Court of Human Rights); and then the third act of violence carried out against his body came when he was automatically made a citizen of the Russian Federation. And there was yet another violation. In May 2018, when he was in the Bely medved' ['White Bear'] penal colony, Sentsov declared a permanent hunger strike, demanding the release of sixty-four Ukrainian political prisoners who were being held in Russia. The prison staff began to force-feed him with a nutritional medicinal mixture, thus not giving him the right to control his own body or to choose to die. Thus, Foucault's classic formula of biopolitics is carried out: after claiming a monopoly on death, the state has now taken over the monopoly on life; as well as the classic enforcement of death (through execution, torture and war), it now holds an enforcement on life.

In Bed with the State

The state's control over the body of the individual is the missing link in the transition from the hybrid regime of the first decade of this century to the open authoritarianism of the second. The politicization of the human body continued throughout the whole of Putin's third term from 2012 to 2018, which was notable for various biopolitical regulations, from the brutal 'Dima Yakovlev Law' of 2012,[9] to the discriminatory law of 2013 that banned any 'promotion of homosexuality among minors' and led to increased violence against representatives of the LGBT community; from the demonstrative destruction of Western foodstuffs that fell foul of Russian 'counter-sanctions',[10] right up to the absurd initiatives of local lawmakers – such as in Chelyabinsk, where they proposed calling up into the army women who had not had any children by the time they were 20 years old. The state tore up the post-Soviet social contract, which was based on non-interference by the authorities in the private lives of its citizens, and which had created a generally modernized, uninhibited and permissive society (albeit one that still harboured gender stereotypes and domestic violence).

By the end of 2010, it seemed that the state was not just coming into our kitchens – and even our refrigerators, dictating what we should eat – but into our bedrooms, too, telling us whom we should sleep with and how many children we should have. But if biopolitics alone was not enough, they added more archaic practices of direct physical coercion. Today's Russia is not just a place where gay parades and foreign adoptions are banned, where they declare sexual sovereignty and moral superiority over the West, it is also a place where they beat schoolchildren, torture people in police stations and prison colonies, and pack people into paddy wagons.

Despite all this, beatings and torture are not directly sanctioned from on high. This is the natural answer of the repressive machine to the state's policy of dealing with the physical body. The archaization of the state's politics and governance reaches into the sphere of the human body, and institutions of Modernity are replaced by the practices of the Middle Ages. Violence starts on TV talk-shows with a mock fight and the staged beating of a Ukrainian (or Polish, or American) guest; it continues with the recruitment by Russian private military companies of mercenaries to fight in Ukraine and in hot spots all over the world, where they are thrown into the meat grinders of local conflicts; and it ends with needles under fingernails and bags over heads in the police station round the corner. The circle closes. Having turned the Russian population into a biological resource, into fodder for the state, into a taxable and recruited mass, the Leviathan does with them the only thing it can do: discipline and punish.

Back to 1937

A perennial topic of discussions among the Russian intelligent-sia has been whether or not we are in 'a new 1937', the year that is synonymous in Russian history with Stalin's 'Great Terror'.[1] Some have pointed to the growing wave of repressions that have been aimed at everyone on the ever-expanding list of victims: the oligarchs, regional governors, *siloviki*, users of social media and the urban middle class. Others disagree, arguing quite reasonably that there have been no mass shootings, and the repressions have been carefully targeted. However, the way in which protests in Moscow were put down by force in the summer of 2019, ahead of the elections to the Moscow City Council, was unprecedented even by Russian standards: hundreds of people were beaten by the police and Rosgvardiya, arms and legs were broken, heads cracked, more than 2,000 people were detained, all the independent candidates in the local elections were arrested and the authorities invented a criminal case about mass riots. All of this speaks of the repressive regime moving to a new level, and one in which we can speak of 'a new 1937' not just metaphorically, but more literally. The season of political terror is now open in Russia.

Punishment of the Innocent

As the philosopher Michail Ryklin noted, in his book *Terrorologics*, the essence of Stalin's Great Terror of 1937–8 was not even its scope, but its absolute and universal nature. It came out of nowhere, like an irresistible external force, like fate in a Greek tragedy, and could go for anyone, whether they were guilty of anything or not. The 'Red Terror' of the Russian Revolution of 1917 and the Civil War that followed from 1918 to 1922 was dreadful but, to some extent, understandable, as at least it had some sort of reasoning behind it (although this is not to justify it). Members of the White movement were shot, as were monarchists, priests, 'the reactionary classes' (the bourgeoisie and landowners) and those who resisted the Revolution (for example, in the revolt of the sailors at Kronstadt in 1921 or the Antonov peasant uprising in the Tambov guberniya in 1920–1). Many innocent people died, but the Red Terror was justified by those who carried it out as being 'demanded by the Revolution'. However, the Great Terror that came after it did not need any reasons, or subjects, or foundations: it simply developed out of the logic of Soviet discourse.

There was a Soviet joke in which a prison guard in the Gulag asked a prisoner what he was in for. 'I didn't do anything', replies the prisoner. 'You lying bastard', says the guard. 'For doing nothing you get ten years. But you're in for fifteen!' This 'ten years for doing nothing' contains the whole meaning of the Great Terror; or, to be more precise, its total lack of meaning. This was terror for its own sake, the pure production of violence, fear and a submissive, paralysed society. The very essence of terror was formulated by the founders of revolutionary terrorism in Russia in the second half of the nineteenth century (in this sense, we could call Russia the birthplace of terrorism). It is the terrorizing of both those in power and the people by the way state officials were systematically killed. Its key characteristic was the unstoppable, total and random nature of the use of violence, meaning that innocent people inevitably suffered. This element of murdering the innocent became even more important in the twentieth century, from the terror of the Bolsheviks, through the Khmer Rouge in Cambodia, and to the Islamic terrorism of the late twentieth and twenty-first centuries. Violence should be both sudden and blind, threatening to rain down on anyone, thus achieving its maximum effect.

I witnessed this myself during a protest in Moscow. I joined a small group of demonstrators who were marching down Strastnoy Boulevard towards the Petrovsky Gates Square. In the middle of a narrow pavement, with their feet wide apart, there stood three 'cosmonauts' (as the riot police have been nicknamed; in their helmets and body armour they look like cosmonauts in their spacesuits). They were filtering the flow of people, and taking it in turns to grab now one, now another. As I approached, I saw them looking at me with a voracious, studied stare from behind their plexiglass visors. It seems that at that moment I was, in the biblical phrase, 'weighed, but found to be too light', and they let me pass. But the young guy with curly hair walking behind me was not so lucky. In an instant, they grabbed him by his arms, twisted them behind his back, and a couple of seconds later he was dragged, bent double, towards the paddy wagon.

Anonymous Violence

Another feature that links the actions of the security forces with Stalin's repressions is the anonymity of the terror. It is carried out in the name of the collective, or the enthusiastic masses, who demand to 'Shoot 'em like mad dogs!', which was a slogan heard frequently at demonstrations and also something that appeared in the so-called 'collective letters' during Stalin's show trials. Like in Soviet times, with their staged meetings of indignant workers at factories and the collective letters of condemnation sent to *Pravda*, a propaganda campaign was waged in the Russian media, in which those who took part in the protests of summer 2019 were described as 'traitors' and demands were made for such demonstrations to be broken up without restraint.

On the other side, too, this terror is anonymous. The police and Rosgvardiya use every means to cover up the faces and identities of their members who break up demonstrations. They wear masks and balaclavas, and they put cling film on the visors of their helmets (this is supposed to distort the face in photographs). Furthermore, Rosgvardiya is not governed by the law on policing, and is permitted to operate anonymously, with no judicial oversight of it. The beatings and tortures in Russian prisons take place in the same anonymous way: the victim is laid face-down on the floor, or they're blindfolded or have a bag placed over their head, so that the torturer's identity often remains unknown. Violence in Russia is spread across the country in a thin layer, faceless and unpunished.

The Semiotics of Terror

Finally, the third comparison with Stalin's repressions is a stylistic one. Terror stalks the streets of Moscow, which have been re-modelled by the mayor, Sergei Sobyanin. It is a city that has been licked clean and lined with granite. Just as the Great Terror unravelled in the stage set of Stalin's reconstruction of Moscow (his General Plan of 1935), so the modern terror has been brought into the recently beautified capital. Social media is full of photographs of the serried ranks of the OMON beside the Operetta Theatre on Bolshaya Dmitrovka Street, decorated with a million LED lamps, a favourite place for Instagram selfies; or columns of Rosgvardiya soldiers near the Moscow Arts Theatre in Kamergersky Lane, marching towards the shocked bronze statue of Anton Chekhov. The 'cosmonauts' form picturesque groups around the granite benches and flower vases, as they drag protesters across the newly laid granite tiles, and knock people off their city-bikes, roughly beating a passing cyclist, the very symbol of the hipster urbanization that Mayor Sobyanin was trying to cultivate. Suddenly it became clear that it was as if these granite pedestrian zones had been created as locations for the totalitarian dystopia performed by Rosgvardiya. On these wide pedestrianized areas, they have somewhere to park their paddy wagons and space to turn around their ranks of stormtroopers. It was not by chance that Georges-Eugène Haussmann (otherwise known as Baron Osman) swept away the old labyrinth of 'the belly of Paris' after the street battles that took place during the Paris Commune in 1871, and in their place designed wide boulevards, where it was difficult to erect barricades but easy to turn troops and artillery. In the same way, the reconstructed centre of Moscow has proved to be a perfect battleground for manoeuvring units of the security forces so that they can practise new tactics for breaking up demonstrations carried out by live, unarmed and defenceless people.

. . . It was late in the evening, when the arrests had already finished, that I drove around the Boulevard Ring Road. It was a Saturday, but the crowds and the usual bustle of summer had been driven from the Boulevard Ring, and the pavement cafes and terraces were all shut; there were no people in the centre of Moscow. Along the whole length of the ring road, among the advertising hoardings, the parking places for the city-bikes and the luridly illuminated trees (thousands of LED lamps had been hung along Moscow's boulevards and in its parks), the only things that were shining were the helmets and shields of the Rosgvardiya soldiers. It was as if the centre of my city had been occupied by aliens, mutant arthropod ants. This post-apocalyptic vision was frightening and heart-stopping.

The semiotics of terror rule in Russia. In Putin's third decade, when the Crimean champagne had gone flat, they decided to replace politics with terror. The authorities' legitimacy is now guaranteed not by mock democracy and elections, but by the truncheons of the OMON and Rosgvardiya. This is an experiment in the deployment of political terror, which was applied in Moscow and can now be spread across the whole of Russia. Sooner or later, it is bound to break out beyond its borders.

The Final Diagnosis

Sometimes it appears that politics in Russia in recent years has been replaced by medicine. In 2020–2, the country has been through the coronavirus pandemic, quarantines and lockdowns, heated arguments about vaccinations and QR codes, and permanent rumours about Putin's health. The president's body, once adored by the media, showing him riding horseback with a naked torso, became an object of public scrutiny, as well as his isolation in a bunker at the height of the pandemic, and the comic 'social distance' he maintained during meetings with foreign leaders, sitting at the far end of a long table.

At the same time, there has been another epidemic raging in Russia: the poisoning plague. In 2015 and 2017, there were two attempts to poison the opposition politician Vladimir Kara-Murza, which he barely survived, after being put into an induced coma. In 2018, in the English city of Salisbury, Sergei Skripal – a former member of the Main Intelligence Directorate of the Russian General Staff, the GRU – and his daughter, Yuliya, were poisoned with a paralysing nerve agent called 'Novichok'. In 2019, an attempt was made to poison the writer and opposition member Dmitry Bykov, with the same substance. And in August 2020, another attempt was made to kill the opposition leader Alexei Navalny, with the ubiquitous Novichok, but by some miracle he survived.

Covid Authoritarianism

In a time of Covid, medicine rules. There was a 'medicalization' of daily life, society, politics and international relations. The political body of the nation became a subject for pathological analysis; healthcare became national security; the arms race became the race for a vaccine; and national sovereignty became collective immunity. Experts and doctors took the place of politicians; the difference was that we did not elect them, our understanding of their area is vague, yet they deal with our lives much more freely than any democratically elected and accountable politician. As an example of this, the whole world looked on at Sweden's chief epidemiologist, Anders Tegnell, who over the course of a year decided the fate of a whole nation with his experimental strategy for doing battle (or, rather, avoiding battle) with the pandemic. Statistics have no less power over society. The late French philosopher Bruno Latour noted that statistics had become the main form of biopolitics in the world today, while the population is regarded as a controlled statistical and pathological mass.

In Russia, coronavirus was embedded in the politics of an authoritarian regime. When the first wave of coronavirus struck in the first half of 2020, the spread of the pandemic coincided with the preparation of the previously planned political reform that was to guarantee Putin unlimited power and the legal right to rule for decades. At first, coronavirus seemed to ruin his Napoleonic plans to rewrite the Constitution and change the political system, particularly in March 2020, when simultaneously the price of oil and the value of the rouble collapsed under the influence of the global lockdown. At that point in the spring, Russia made some attempts to manage the epidemic by applying international standards. There were partial quarantines and lockdowns, one-off payments were made to families with many children, and measures were announced to support business and reduce debt (which, incidentally, few were able to take advantage of). However, overall, these measures amounted to about 2 per cent of Russia's GDP, at a time when the developed countries were spending 20 per cent and higher.

By the summer of 2020, the first wave had died down, and it seemed to the authorities that the epidemic was under control, and that the population had not expressed any particular dissatisfaction, neither about the catastrophic lack of medical support in the regions, nor about the loss of wages that the crisis had caused. So it was decided that the national vote on the Constitution could go ahead. The epidemic was used as a political instrument to test the format of an early vote, held over several days (with serious restrictions on the possibilities for having independent observers). Using the excuse of public health measures, the ballot boxes were placed in the boots of cars, in courtyards of buildings and, in the countryside, even on tree-stumps. All through those months, protest continued to be suppressed, citing health reasons, so by the end of the first year of the pandemic, Russia was faced with a complete ban on street activity, be it demonstrations or single-person pickets.

Masks Off

The Covid pandemic has shown yet another element of Russian society and its political culture: a disregard for human life and safety. Except for a short period of strict lockdown in the spring of 2020, the majority of the population has shown a remarkable disrespect for wearing masks, quarantines and social distancing; moreover, Russia has seen some record numbers of Covid-dissidents and anti-vaxxers. The popular argument for this sounded Darwinian: 'If you're going to fall ill, you'll fall ill; if you're going to die, you'll die.' A new cynical social agreement appeared that seemed to suit everyone: the authorities gave the impression that they were fighting Covid, and the population gave the impression that they were following public health rules;[1] the whole of Russia was wearing a mask under its chin in the 'Get lost!' style.

This was less an epidemiological diagnosis than a social one: the immunodeficiency of society and low social capital. The basis of this capital is trust, and a mask is a sign of solidarity with your fellow citizens; the higher the social capital in a society, the more readily people wear masks. The fact that wearing masks was so unpopular in Russia was an indicator of a lack of trust (in the authorities by the citizens, and among the citizens themselves), a sign of social atomization and of a fragmented and embittered society.

This dislike of masks has also revealed the extreme disregard that Russians have for their lives and their health. This is a paternalistic, dependent society, where for centuries the state has removed responsibility from the individual, and yet where life was exposed to multiple risks, from a harsh climate to wars, from rampant crime to oppression by the state. As a result, the individual has developed a disdainful attitude to life, both their own and that of others. This accounts for the myths that have arisen about Russian daring and Russian courage; but it is also the source of recklessness, a disrespect for rules, and the suicidal drinking habits among the population.

A fair comparison with the issue of masks is that of seatbelts in cars. You would think that these days it would not be necessary to convince anyone of the usefulness of seatbelts in saving lives. Yet to this day there are still many drivers in Russia who will fasten their seatbelt behind their back, to avoid the annoyance of the reminder alert from the car; and for these purposes you can buy a typical Russian invention – a silencer for the seatbelt safety alert: a piece of metal that you put into the seatbelt lock instead of the seatbelt itself, to prevent the car from sounding the seatbelt warning. Research carried out by the State Automobile Inspectorate in the autumn of 2019 showed that, across the whole of Russia, only about two-thirds of drivers put on their seatbelt. In this sense, there is an equally dangerous pathogen stalking Russia along with coronavirus: the virus of irresponsibility and neglect of human life.

Bare Life

The medicalization of politics reached its peak in the summer of 2020, when, against the background of the passing of a new Constitution and consolidation of Putin's personal dictatorship, the decision was made to bring about a 'final solution' to the problem of the opposition leader, Alexei Navalny. In August 2020, when Navalny was visiting the Siberian city of Tomsk, agents from a special detachment of the FSB put Novichok in his clothing in the hotel where he was staying. On his return flight to Moscow, the politician fell ill and started to expire, but an emergency landing was made in another Siberian city, Omsk, where paramedics from the ambulance service carried out successful emergency procedures that saved his life. According to the original plan, the aircraft should have flown straight to Moscow, where specially prepared medical staff from the FSB would not have allowed him to live. For two days, the Kremlin repeatedly refused to grant permission for him to leave the country. But then Navalny, in an artificially induced coma, was taken to Berlin in a special container, where, over the course of a month, doctors in the Charité Clinic managed to save his life.

What had been conceived as a special operation by poisoners and pre-prepared doctors unexpectedly went wrong and turned into a major blunder by the FSB, causing international outrage. A detailed account of the patient's illness from the Charité Clinic was published in the journal *The Lancet*, which infuriated the Kremlin. Visibly annoyed, the Russian President's press secretary, Dmitry Peskov, remarked that 'We don't read medical publications.'

For many weeks, reports about the condition of 'the Berlin patient' – as they referred to him in the Kremlin because they were too afraid to say his name – held Russian society transfixed. As the details unfolded about the poisoning, Navalny was brought to the forefront of world politics. This was confirmed when the then German chancellor, Angela Merkel, visited him in hospital. From that moment, Navalny was not just an opposition politician in a provincial dictatorship, but a figure of global stature, who could yet climb to the heights of Vaclav Havel or Nelson Mandela. His brave return to Russia in January 2021, arrest on the border, imprisonment, and the list of subsequent charges (the latest of which, in March 2022, has seen him sentenced to a further nine years in prison) have made him into Russia's main political prisoner. The images of his gaunt body in Prison Colony No. 6 near the town of Pokrov in Vladimir Oblast, where he is tortured by unbearable conditions and is constantly being shut away in solitary confinement, have become a symbol of resistance in Russia.

The attempt to destroy Alexei Navalny's body has given him special rights: 'the Berlin patient', and now 'the Pokrov prisoner', stands alongside 'the Kremlin patient', who was isolated in his bunker for most of the pandemic. And if, previously, Russian politics was focused solely on the body of Vladimir Putin (like in medieval political theology, as described by the historian Ernst Kantorovich, 'the body of the king' becomes the political body of the nation), now it is also linked to the body of Alexei Navalny – in a hospital bed, in a courthouse cage and in a solitary confinement cell – a tortured, yet undefeated, body.

The tendency to 'medicalize' has brought the biological, organic contours of the human body to the forefront of politics. In the era of the virtual and the digital, politics suddenly becomes physical once more, touching questions of life and death, the very edge of human existence. Under the pretext of the battle against the pandemic, the state declared a 'state of emergency', placing itself above the law and the norm – and our existence was turned into 'bare life' that is worth nothing, like in a concentration camp. A person can be poisoned with no punishment forthcoming, judged without any evidence being presented, have drugs planted on them, be accused of extremism or have their life torn to shreds. This is exactly how, a hundred years ago, based on the ideas of 'blood and soil', and through the manifestation and repression of a person's physicality, fascism was born in Europe.

People as 'The New Oil'

The first day of September is a special one in the Russian calendar. Known as 'the Day of Knowledge', when the school year begins, it is regarded as a carnival of fruitfulness and of love for our offspring. It is marked by splendid bouquets and the children lining up in a ceremonial parade in schoolyards. An indispensable part of the ritual involves various big-wigs visiting schools. This year, President Putin himself blessed schoolchildren in Vladivostok with his presence. His lecture (as usual, about history; just as Stalin wrote articles about linguistics, so Putin will go down on record as an amateur historian) began with a curious misunderstanding. One of the pupils asked Putin to *sign up* to his YouTube channel, but the president thought that he was being asked to *sign* something. This illustrated the cultural gulf between the young, digital, generation, and the elderly bureaucrat of the era of paper, who does not use the Internet (as he has frequently admitted) and signs documents that are brought to him in files.

The main news, however, was about not history but demography. Putin declared that, had the Russian state not collapsed twice, in 1917 and 1991, 'then our population would be almost 500 million'. Just for the record: according to the latest census, the Russian population is 147 million, a figure that is rapidly decreasing.

500 Million Serfs

This dream of 500 million people follows Putin around. In his televised address to the nation in June 2021, he mistakenly said that 500 million Russians had taken advantage of preferential mortgages, which became an inexhaustible source of jokes. This figure of 500 million has come up before in official statements. Back in 2012, the then deputy prime minister, Dmitry Rogozin, called on Russians to have more children, claiming that, without it, 'we won't have the 500 million-strong population that we so desperately need'.

It is typical that the president sees the reason for the shortfall in the population as being the collapse of two empires, and not the crimes of Bolshevism: not the deaths of the victims of the 'Red Terror' and the Civil War of 1918–22, nor the three waves of famine in 1921–2, 1932–3 and 1946–7 (in which up to 13 million people perished); not because of the collectivization of the 1930s, nor the deportation of whole peoples in the 1940s; it was not (in Putin's view) anything to do with the 'Great Terror' of 1937–8, or the post-War repressions . . . Even if one is sceptical of the figure of 66.7 million people eliminated by the state (not counting the War) put forward by Alexander Solzhenitsyn, we are nevertheless talking about tens of millions of people. All of them were the victims of state policy – about which, however, President Putin chooses to remain silent. For him, the tragedy lies not in the state's terror, but in the collapse of statehood and the loss of territory.

This magical figure of a population of half a billion is rooted in the logic of 'resources' that Russian power stands on. The Russian sociologist Simon Kordonsky has described Russia as 'a resource state', in which policy is built around the development, appropriation and redistribution of resources. Everything – not just raw materials – is turned into a resource. Power, state services, informal connections, information, violence, threats: these are all considered to be resources. This archaic logic of resources demands not only more oil, timber and coal, but more territory – hence all the plans for territory held by Putin's regime, from Russia's megalomaniac claim on the 1.2 million square kilometres of the Arctic, including the area around the North Pole, to the local military operations to seize land from its neighbours – the Crimea and eastern provinces from Ukraine; Abkhazia and South Ossetia from Georgia – and discussions about the unification of Belarus with Russia. Putin's claims in 2020 that, when the Soviet Union was created, many of the republics that became a part of it 'received a huge amount of Russian land' and 'historically traditional Russian territories' were made in the same archaic paradigm of territorial thinking. What is more, the Russian president believes that, when these republics left the USSR, they should have 'left with what they had when they joined', and that they should not have 'taken with them presents from the Russian people'. These declarations have seriously worried Russia's neighbours – first and foremost, Kazakhstan.

The population is just another resource at the disposal of the state, which governs them with the aid of what Michel Foucault calls biopower. As the political scientist Kirill Martynov has noted:

Foucault would be delighted with President Putin as an example of a nineteenth-century political leader brought back to life 200 years later, who thinks along the lines of 'population, territory and security'. For this reason, people are needed, so that there are workers ('the foundation of statehood'), soldiers and prison guards; this is how a strong state reproduces itself in the bodies of its subjects.

The prison guards, incidentally, are already being actively cloned. A specialized class opened at School No. 67 in Novosibirsk on 1 September 2022, which will prepare the senior classes to enter the FSIN [prison service] training colleges. There are FSIN classes in schools in other parts of the country that are known for their prison colonies: in Irkutsk Oblast, Mordovia, Krasnoyarsk Region and Bashkortostan.

Living to Pension Age

This resource logic dictated the raising of the pension age in Russia in 2018, from 55 to 60 for women, and from 60 to 65 for men. When we consider that in 2017 the average life expectancy of a man in Russia was only 67 (a record low indicator for developed countries), many men risk not even reaching retirement age. The pension reform was hugely unpopular in Russia – on more than one occasion during his time in office Putin had promised not to raise the pension age – and in one stroke halved the president's rating among senior citizens, his most loyal electorate. Nevertheless, the government went down this route, having come up against a shortfall in the Pension Fund, an ageing population, and a shortage of labour.

As the forage base of a resource state decreases and the subsoil is depleted, it is people who become 'the new oil', like a hydrocarbon, a biomass. They must be compelled to be more productive and efficient, by raising the pension age, and privatizing ever more social benefits that are a legacy of the USSR, from education to healthcare. There is plenty of evidence of this attitude in the ruling class of treating the people as a resource in the many remarks made by Russian officials, advising the population to live and eat more modestly. These range from the classic words of the Prime Minister, Dmitry Medvedev: 'There's no money, but just hang in there'; to the declaration by Olga Glatskikh, a member of the government of

Sverdlovsk Oblast: 'In principle, the state owes you nothing'; and to the suggestion by Natalya Sokolova, the minister of labour for Saratov Oblast, to her voters that they could feed themselves for 3,500 roubles (50 dollars) a month: 'The price of noodles doesn't change.'

Following the logic of biopolitics, the state is building a pro-birth demographic policy: paying maternity benefit; removing abortion from the state insurance system (in all likelihood, abortion will soon be banned and criminalized); proposing a tax on childlessness, and preferential mortgages for large families. The population is being encouraged to multiply – an intrusive advertising campaign by housing developers encourages people to breed in the concrete cages of the new residential complexes. The corrupt union of local authorities, developers and insatiable construction firms is leading to concrete circles of skyscrapers shooting up in Russian cities like human anthills, in which the population is busy creating more taxpayers, soldiers and future mothers.

Dead Souls

At the same time, the state apparatus does not hold back from traditional Russian practices, such as fixing data, distorting the figures and falsifying statistics. A typical example of this was the 2021 population census. There are multiple independent witness accounts that illustrate that the census-takers visited barely a quarter of all households. The rest of the data was simply taken from the registration books in places of residence, from the Government Services website and from other administrative registers, where the information was either out of date or simply made up. In certain regions, results were invented in a competition between governors, in the same way as with election results, because the head of each region tries to present the Kremlin with the most encouraging figures.

So, for example, the head of Bashkortostan, Radiy Khabirov, announced that 4,100,000 citizens of the republic participated in the All-Russian Census . . . despite the fact that in January 2021 the population of Bashkortostan was under 4 million. The point was that Khabirov wanted to out-do the president of the neighbouring republic of Tatarstan, Rustam Minnikhanov. These two regions turned the census into a contest between the two of them.

Specialists in this field warn observers to be especially wary of data from the Caucasus, where traditionally there is a high percentage of pseudo-pensioners, pseudo-invalids and others who receive social benefits, thanks to falsified figures and certificates. Incidentally, this helps to explain the myth about 'the longevity of Caucasian people'. It is not uncommon for someone to be issued with a false birth certificate: so, when you reach 25, hey presto! suddenly you're a 70-year-old pensioner! Generally speaking, figures from the State Federal Statistics Service (Rosstat) do not correspond with social or demographic data, they are purely administrative and political markers, adjusted to suit the existing tasks of the authorities, for planning guidance and as part of the administrative battle for budget resources. As Simon Kordonsky has put it, Russian state statistics still follow Soviet logic: 'Usually a census is a way of counting the population. The Soviet census was a way of controlling the population.'[1]

According to his observations, a little while ago when the Russian *siloviki* counted up the figures from the registry offices (they digitized all the data on births and deaths from registry offices across the territory of the Russian Federation and worked out the number of people living), they came up with a figure of 90 million. On the other hand, there are a huge number of people in the country who cannot be accounted for, such as migrants, rural dwellers who seek work in the towns and seasonal labourers. Then there are whole settlements of people who do not appear in the statistics. They do not have a postcode, they are not on the electricity grid, they are not linked up in any way; in reality, the state has no hold over them. Judicially, they do not exist – you will not find them on any map; yet they are real people. Therefore, Kordonsky says, you have to be very wary when using figures from Rosstat, including when it comes to the size of the population: 'Maybe we don't have 145,000,000 people, maybe it's 120 million. Or maybe it's 160,000,000. God alone knows.'

As a result, Russians live in a country where, to go with your moonshine vodka, your 'cheese-like product' (as the cheese substitute is called that is being made in Russia because of the food counter-sanctions), the spoof doping-samples of Russian athletes, the forged statistics about Covid and the fake QR codes for vaccinations, there is now a fabricated population census. Its results give insufficient information about Russian society, but bear witness to the deep crisis in the Russian state. This has been written about frequently in Russian literature, most notably in Nikolai Gogol's immortal *Dead Souls*, the most important book about Russia. Almost 200 years after it was written, dead souls are filling up Russian statistics and giving the leadership fantasies about their own power and the number of subjects beneath them.

Superfluous People

Behind this game with the figures, no one is asking the most obvious questions: why does Russia need a population of half a billion, and where are they going to live? In the ghost towns of the Far North, that have become a complete socio-economic disaster? In the Far East? No one wants to go and live there (despite the state promising a free hectare of land to any new arrival) and people are leaving the area in droves. In the less fertile, non-black earth territories in Central Russia? But there is a similar exodus taking place there, which is turning it into a land of dead villages and dying small towns. Can the infrastructure of Russian towns, the water resources, the recycling plants, cope with these new people? To what extent is Russian healthcare ready for this influx, when in the Covid pandemic its failings were there for all to see?

And, finally, the main question: does mankind need new people? Should we really be pressing for a thoughtless increase in human lives when poverty and inequality are increasing on the planet; when the Earth does not have sufficient resources; when we cannot guarantee to future generations that they will have clean air, fresh water, biodiversity or a climate that can sustain life? What is the most important thing for a modern state: the number of subjects it has or the quality of life? In post-industrial societies that have been through the 'second demographic transition', people are wealthier and live longer, and give birth to fewer children, and later in life, than was the case in traditional societies; and individuals choose for themselves a life with a family or on their own. The aim of politics should not be to increase the birth rate and the size of the population, but to lower mortality rates, increase the longevity and the quality of life, improve healthcare and social welfare . . .

But all these questions succumb to the demographic utopia and the resource logic of a state for whom people are simply a natural raw material, 'the new oil'; they are too complex for the archaic thinking that confuses signing up to YouTube with signing a decree.

The Zoos of Terror

Chechen *siloviki* are once again ruling the roost in Central Russia. In Nizhny Novgorod on 20 January 2022, they grabbed Zaryema Musayeva, the mother of the lawyer from the Committee Against Torture, Abubakar Yangulbayev. The woman was taken from her apartment still wearing her house clothes, without her shoes (there are images of them leading her barefoot over the snow) and without her essential medication (she is diabetic).

The Yangulbayev case has been going on for many years. The father, Saydi Yangulbayev, made his career in the investigative and judicial bodies of the Chechen Republic, and became a member of the Supreme Court of Chechnya. At the same time, his sons, Abubakar and Ibrahim, were writing on social networks about the history of Chechnya and about violations of human rights, and they criticized the republic's leadership. In November 2015, the ruler of Chechnya, Ramzan Kadyrov, had the father and the two sons brought to his residence. There, the men were beaten brutally, and forced to lick up their own blood off the floor. After this, the father and one son were released, but Ibrahim was detained for a further six months in the basement of a local police station. Abubakar continued writing his critical reports and became the lawyer for the Committee Against Torture. Towards the end of 2021, his relatives in Chechnya, some fifty of them, started to disappear; then his apartment in the town of Pyatigorsk was searched. The father and both sons fled Russia and are now in hiding abroad. When they learnt this, the Chechen *siloviki* grabbed the sons' mother, Zaryema Musayeva, brought false charges of fraud against her and are still holding her in prison. The fate of the other relatives is unknown.

This special operation by these Chechen *siloviki* in regions of the Russian Federation that are far from Chechnya was not a one-off. They regularly seize people across the whole of Russia. A year earlier, the Chechen police had taken two brothers, Magamadov and Isayev, one of whom was gay, the other transgender. In September 2020 in Gelendzhik in the Krasnodar territory, the moderator of the Chechen Telegram channel 1ADAT, Salman Tepsurkayev, was grabbed; in May 2021, at the Novogireyevo metro station in Moscow, Chechen thugs seized Ibrahim Selimkhanov, a Dagestani and another representative of the LGBT community. However, the seizure of Zaryema Musayeva caused a particular stir, so much so that President Putin's press secretary, Dmitry Peskov, was forced to comment on it. At first, he described the story as 'fantasy'; then he was forced to retract this. Finally, Peskov responded to the statement made by Kadyrov that 'either a place in prison, or a place under the ground awaits' the Yangulbayev family, and that, should they resist capture, they should be 'destroyed': Peskov called this 'Citizen Kadyrov's personal opinion'. Peskov's obvious cowardice demonstrates the clear fact that Chechnya is untouchable across the whole territory of the Russian Federation, and is exempt from the Russian Constitution and legal system, as well as from Putin's criticism.

Under Ramzan Kadyrov, Chechnya itself was long ago turned into a medieval khanate, based on executions, torture and terror. In March 2021, the US State Department issued a report on human rights violations in Russia, in which they described twenty kinds of human rights violations – covering just the major ones – carried out by the local authorities in Chechnya. They reported mass illegal executions, including those of gays; violent abductions of people; and tortures carried out by members of the law enforcement bodies in secret prisons in the Chechen Republic. The report also included murders carried out beyond the boundaries of Chechnya and the Russian Federation that were thought to be linked to Kadyrov's people. There was the murder of Imran Aliev in France in January 2020, and of Mamikhan Umarov in Austria in July that year.[1] The Russian newspaper *Novaya gazeta* has frequently written about executions and torture in Chechnya, such as the extra-legal execution in 2017 of twenty-seven people, allegedly for their part in the attack on a police station in Grozny in December 2016. Before their deaths, the accused were brutally tortured and forced on camera to swear their allegiance to the Islamic State. And this is not limited just to murdering Kadyrov's enemies. The Chechen authorities also terrorize their families and burn down the homes of their relatives.

All of these barbaric actions that take place on the territory of Chechnya and beyond pass without any reaction from the federal authorities. Even the most notable political assassination in the history of modern Russia, the shooting by the walls of the Kremlin of the leading opposition politician Boris Nemtsov, on 27 February 2015 – the roots of which led to the highest leadership in Chechnya – was not fully investigated. The court restricted itself to the formal charging and punishment of those who carried out the crime, but who it was that ordered the murder was never established. When representatives of the Investigative Committee and the Russian FSB arrived in the Chechen capital of Grozny to carry out an investigation, they were not even allowed to leave the airport.

Similar immunity on the territory of Russia is granted to Belarusian law enforcers. After the brutal crackdown on the protests that took place in Belarus in August 2020, they have been hunting for opponents of Alexander Lukashenko's regime who fled to Russia. At least twenty members of the opposition have been captured and returned to Belarus. Some of them, like the journalist from the newspaper *Komsomolskaya pravda v Belarusi* Gennady Mozheyko, were kidnapped and taken back to Minsk; others, such as the former investigator Andrei Ostapovich, were left on the border of Belarus, with a bag over their head and weights chained to their hands, and left for the Belarusian KGB to pick up. These operations set up by the Belarusian *siloviki* go way beyond any judicial procedures and inter-state agreements, and are an infringement of the Russian Federation's sovereignty.

In many ways, Belarus is like Chechnya, in that an exceedingly cruel personal dictatorship has been established there, which terrorizes the population and extensively violates human rights. Over the course of the almost thirty years of Lukashenko's rule since 1994, many of his opponents – and even his former allies – have simply disappeared, such as Viktor Gonchar and Anatoly Krasovsky, Yury Zakharenko and Yury Korban, and many others. There are believed to be over 1,000 political prisoners in Belarus, including nearly all the opposition leaders and anyone who has challenged Lukashenko in elections (such as Viktor Babariko, Maria Kolesnikova and Sergei Tikhanovsky). The death penalty is used in Belarus: since 1990, over 400 people have been shot. After the protests in 2020, tens of thousands of people went through the notorious investigation chambers at Zhodino and Okrestina, and many of them were tortured.

In this context, we should also remember the criminal regimes installed in the Donetsk and Luhansk Oblasts of Ukraine that Russia has occupied, as well as Crimea, annexed by Russia in 2014. In the self-proclaimed 'people's republics' of Donetsk and Luhansk, property is simply taken; people disappear; illegal detentions and torture are widely practised in the terrifying cellars of the police and the state security bodies; men are captured on the street and sent to the front. In Crimea, which Russia considers to be its own territory, a special legal regime has been enforced. Hundreds of political prisoners have been seized, journalists and activists are followed, any Ukrainians who remain there are persecuted, and Crimean Tatars suffer repressions that show symptoms of ethnic cleansing. In fact, Russia has established a *cordon anti-sanitaire*, a belt of lawless regimes along its southern boundary, from Chechnya and the non-recognized republics of the Caucasus (Abkhazia and South Ossetia), through Donetsk, Luhansk and Crimea to Belarus.

There are two openly terrorist regimes that stand out in this belt, Chechnya and Belarus: one a subject of the Russian Federation, the other a part of the Union State of Russia and Belarus. These are two territories that are outside the legal order and are run with the aid of terror. This can seem excessive, even against the background of the authoritarian, police regime in Russia. Some even say that they challenge the Kremlin – but it's not like that at all. In reality, they fit reliably into the political system of the Russian Federation as 'wildlife reservations' – or, perhaps more accurately, as 'zoos of terror'. They appear to be unpredictable and uncontrollable, but they are actually sponsored by Moscow (we're talking here about tens of billions of dollars); they know exactly the boundaries they can go to, and they understand where the money and the resources come from. These are showgrounds for demonstrative cruelty, rather like ancient Roman circuses, where lions tormented the early Christians. And the indifference (in the Chechen case) and favour (in the Belarusian) with which the Russian authorities regard the way in which their travelling *siloviki* operate on Russian territory confirms that they are part of the Russian political terror machine.

They say that Ramzan Kadyrov has a home zoo in his palace in Grozny (a residence larger than the Winter Palace in St Petersburg), with lions, tigers and crocodiles. This zoo plays exactly the same role in frightening his enemies as Chechnya itself and Belarus play in the Russian Federation's political system: it is a zoo of terror, that occasionally is allowed to go on tour on the streets of Russian towns, and has now escaped beyond the boundary of Russia.

The Generator of Entropy

The Russian president is renowned for his professional habit of lying; but occasionally he demonstrates surprising openness. At a meeting of the collegium of the Ministry of Foreign Affairs at the end of 2021, he declared that a 'certain tension' had arisen in the West because of Russia's actions, and that the aim of Russia's policy was 'that this situation remains so for as long as possible'. Perhaps he did not intend to do so, but in saying this Vladimir Putin revealed the essence and the method of Russian foreign policy: to support tension in the outside world. If, previously, the leaders of the USSR spoke (perhaps rhetorically) about lessening international tension, now the country's president claims that tension is his main instrument.

A couple of days later, one of the main ideologues of the Kremlin and the former assistant to the president, Vladislav Surkov, eloquently developed the thoughts of his patron, when he published his article, 'Where Has Chaos Gone? Unpacking Instability'. In this, he stresses that Russia should become 'an exporter of chaos' to the outside world. According to Surkov, Russia should use the entropy accumulated in the country, and 'export it for use on a foreign territory'. And in a foreign policy manifesto, typically entitled 'The World Storm and Russian Courage',[1] the pro-Kremlin analyst Sergei Karaganov suggests that Russia should carry out a psychological attack, generating all the same unpredictability and risk. It seems that Russia has positioned itself not only as a force that is prepared for the era of increasing chaos and random behaviour, but also as one of the generators of this chaos.

The Crisis of Russian Soft Power

Such declarations are evidence of strategic weakness. Because Russia is incapable of guaranteeing peace, cooperation and stability, it has begun to specialize in the production of tension as a way of promoting itself, raising its global status and scaring off any opponents. The country's problem is that, by the 2020s, it had exhausted nearly all the traditional attributes of its soft power.[2] The classical forms of Russian cultural exports that hail back to the second half of the nineteenth and the twentieth centuries, which included the Soviet triad of art, sport and science, have been eroded over the past decades. And even though the eternal masterpieces such as the novels of Leo Tolstoy or Tchaikovsky's symphonies remain the calling cards of Russian culture, contemporary culture is poorly represented on the world stage. If we take key figures of international renown, such as the film director Andrei Zvyagintsev, the writer Vladimir Sorokin, the opera director Vladimir Chernyakov or the conductor Vladimir Yurovsky, it turns out that they all now live and work outside Russia.

Another traditional attribute of Soviet and Russian soft power, sporting achievement, has also been devalued in the twenty-first century. A series of doping scandals, above all the exposure of a huge state-run doping programme at the Winter Olympics in Sochi in 2014, led to the International Olympic Committee banning the Russian team from the Games in Rio in 2016, Pyeongchang in 2018, and the Tokyo 2020 Games (which were actually held in 2021).

In a similar way, the third aspect of Soviet soft power, achievements in science and technology, including the leading Space and nuclear programmes, and successes in physics and mathematics, have all remained back in the twentieth century. In the more than thirty years that have passed since the collapse of the USSR, Russia has lost much of its scientific potential and now lies in forty-seventh place in the Global Innovation Index. Over the course of these three decades, just three Russians have won Nobel Prizes; what's more, two of those were for discoveries made in Soviet times. There are now no Nobel laureates for science living in Russia.

The Russian Space programme, which is based on the technology of the 1960s to the 1980s, serves as an example of how far Russia has fallen behind. The technology still works, but is ageing and becoming expensive to maintain, and it is clearly losing out in competition with private business. In terms of efficiency, Elon Musk's company, SpaceX, which employs 8,000 people, beats hands down the Roskosmos Corporation, with its 240,000 employees. The International Space Station is going to close down in 2024 (its life-cycle having twice been extended from the original end of its service that was due in 2015). This will mean that Russia will be left without a permanent presence in Space. Thus, over the past three decades, the traditional Russian resources of soft power, from culture and sports to scientific and technological achievements, have been undermined.[3]

The Export of Fear

So now it becomes clear that Russia has been left with just one more element of its unseen soft power, which is closely connected to its cultural and historical resources: and this is fear. Russia has been a rival of the West for centuries (just think of the Cossack bivouacs on the Champs-Élysées in 1814, and the Soviet tank armies in the centre of Europe from 1945 to 1994), but has now become an existential threat, deeply written into the West's collective memory. In his classic work, the Norwegian political scientist Iver Neumann described Russia as 'Europe's constitutive "Other"';[4] and the Russo-German philosopher Boris Groys, applying the paradigm of psycho-analysis to relations between Russia and the West, suggested that Russia is the West's subconscious, a formless, unconscious Id to which traumas, a sense of threat and fear were displaced.[5]

Today's Russia cannot boast of its military might or its place on the global stage as the Soviet Union could, but it can still play on the fears that lie in Europe's collective memory. Across the ocean, the American collective consciousness also distinctly remembers the Communist threat during the Cold War: 'The Russians are coming!' Continuing this thread, Russia cunningly manipulates these fears, selectively carrying out special operations abroad. Poisoning political opponents and defectors, trying to interfere in elections in various coun-tries, attacks by hackers and 'troll factories' on websites and social networks: in all such cases, official representatives deny that Russia is behind them, but there is a strong consensus in Western public opinion that it is the Russian authorities that are responsible for these operations. A toxic image of an omnipresent and invisible threat has emerged, one that can spring up always and everywhere, and remains unidentified and unpunished. This toxicity is a new version of the classic 'Russian threat' that is very effective in today's world, and it makes up a crucial component of Russia's soft power. It is no longer there to attract friends; it is there to scare off rivals.

Agents of Chaos

So it is not economic, military or diplomatic might; it is not the attractiveness of its social model; it is not its scientific or innovative potential; but it is tension, unpredictability and chaos that have remained as the last trump cards of this nuclear state, with which it can endlessly raise the stakes in the game of confrontation with the West. Soberly weighing up the level of its geopolitical influence and its prospects, Russia uses the hybrid, the indeterminate and risk as instruments of its foreign policy.

For a long time, since the middle of the first decade of this century, Putin's regime has been in a state of sluggish, undeclared war with the West. They dreamt up this idea themselves; and they created it through propaganda, strengthened by a militaristic ideology and the myth of 'the Victory', and provided it with an ever increasing military budget. Even though this war was dreamt up, this did not make it any less real or dangerous; and, in line with the Kremlin's thinking, it had to end with a hot war in which Russia is bound to be victorious, according to the behests of the mythical 'grandfathers'.

This became a strategy of asymptotically approaching the line of conflict and practising the art of brinkmanship, the export of chaos and the creation of zones of tension. This was shown by the prolongation of conflicts, and the creation along the southern and western perimeters of Russia of the aforementioned *cordon anti-sanitaire* – from Abkhazia and South Ossetia (plus now the renewed conflict in Karabakh), through Crimea, the Donbas and Transnistria to Belarus. Here, the terrorist regime of Alexander Lukashenko has already been blackmailing Europe for years, now with floods of migrants, now with shutting off oil and gas pipelines or road transit. For Russia, Belarus has become a political template. Lukashenko was the first to build an authoritarian dictatorship, and the first to unleash a regime of mass repression, and he was also giving Moscow a master class in generating tension and provoking chaos on the border, to persuade Europe to open a dialogue. Moscow is receiving similar lessons in blackmailing from Kim Jong-un in the East, and the regime in Teheran to the South.

In an attempt to create tension around the world, Russia is sending out its agents of chaos. Poisoners from the FSB and military intelligence, the GRU, carried out the attacks on Alexander Litvinenko and Sergei and Yuliya Skripal in Britain. Mercenaries from the Russian private military company Wagner caused disturbances in Syria, Libya and the Central African Republic, and are now fighting in Ukraine. Russian spies blew up an arms depot in the Czech village of Vrbětice in 2014 and attempted a coup in Montenegro in 2016. Hackers from the Kremlin's cyber forces attacked critical infrastructure and the servers of the Democratic Party in the USA, and secret sponsors financed the ultra-right Rassemblement National [the National Rally, formerly the National Front – Tr.] in France, and the Alternative für Deutschland (AfD) in Germany. Then there are the correspondents of the state TV channel, *Russia Today* (RT), spreading fake news about coronavirus in Europe; and the football hooligans brought in from Moscow especially to provoke trouble at the European Football Championships in Marseille in 2016 . . . In November 2021, the Russian Ministry of Defence carried Russian chaos into Space. By inexpertly destroying an old Russian satellite whilst experimenting with an anti-satellite weapon, the military created a cloud of 1,500 shards at orbital height, which presented such a threat to all piloted spaceflight that the International Space Station altered its trajectory and prepared the crew for evacuation.

At the start of 2022, when Russia began to ramp up its groups of forces on the border with Ukraine, preparing for an all-out war, the production of chaos and risk was taken to a new level. Just a few weeks passed before the 'export of tension' that Putin spoke about at the end of 2021 became the export of death.

PART II

THE MEMORY CRUSADE

Kolyma by the Kremlin

An Identity Crisis

A few years have passed since the Zaryadye Park opened close to the Moscow Kremlin. Since then, it has become a part of the Moscow scenery, a must-see on the tourist itinerary, and its 'Soaring Bridge', which hangs like a wing over the Moskva River, has become the most popular selfie spot in the capital. Zaryadye is a signature project for the authorities, as the territory around the Kremlin is considered sacred, and Vladimir Putin himself graced the opening of the park with his presence in 2017. And yet I did not bother to visit, scared away by crowds of onlookers and tourists. An opportunity arose when an old acquaintance of mine from London, who had worked in Moscow in the 1990s but had not been there for twenty years, came on a visit, and I took him along so that we could both marvel at this urban wonder.

It was a gloomy, early autumnal day: the skies hung low over the Kremlin; the wind carried along shreds of cloud. It was busy and noisy in the park. The visitors followed the tricky terrain that was meant to portray all of Russia's different climatic zones. They climbed over the hills and the rocks, calling out to each other before freezing in bizarre poses for photographs. It would appear that the upper part of the park was meant to represent the tundra, a predominant landscape in a country where two-thirds of the territory is covered with permafrost. The dwarf birch trees faintly rustled their leaves, the elfin cedar clung to the ground, timid shoots of vegetation stretched upwards towards the September sky. Despite the presence of rope fences, paths had been roughly trodden into the lawns; here and there, monstrous underground ventilation pipes stuck up out of the ground, looking like tubes from hell. Close to them stood a bunch of fir trees that appeared to be fearfully clinging to each other amid all this chaos. Speakers hidden amongst the branches carried the trilling of nightingales. Security guards in black masks wandered amidst these fragments of nature and civilization, and workers in yellow vests scurried about, constantly wiping things. It was as if we had stumbled upon the building site of disassembled nature on the day before its creation, when there was yet to be any harmony or beauty, just confusion and restlessness.

We continued down to the Kremlin Embankment, where what appeared to be the central Russian landscape was displayed: there was a pond that seemed to have been taken from Ivan Turgenev's novels about the nobility, sprawling willows, and lowland with reeds. Beneath us, on the Embankment itself, and just a couple of steps away, there stood the usual traffic jam, spewing out exhaust fumes. We took our place in the queue for the 'Soaring Bridge', eventually stepping onto it, and, standing there above the turbulent waters of the Moskva River, it struck me that this hanging arc was a metaphor for the whole park: it is a handsome yet pointless bridge to nowhere, a platform for tourists to take selfies against the background of the main symbols of Russian power – the Kremlin and the Cathedral of Christ the Saviour. It could have been extended across the river to the Raushskaya Embankment and the historic, nineteenth-century Hydroelectric Power Station Number One, rather like the Millennium Bridge across the River Thames in London, which leads to the Tate Modern Gallery; but the deliberately foreshortened bridge merely underlines how unnatural and imagined the whole park is.

Finally, we sat on the steps of the open amphitheatre under a silver cupola that covered the hill like a bizarre flying saucer, and consumed 'the very same' Soviet *plombir* ice cream in little wafer cups, which we purchased from a 1950s-style cart.[1] Instead of the trilling of the nightingales, rousing Soviet songs boomed out from the speakers. Down below there was an empty stage, behind which stood bushes and frail trees of the forest-tundra; and through their stunted branches, as if in a post-apocalyptic vision, we could see the domes of St Basil's Cathedral and the Kremlin walls in the disturbing light of sunset. I remembered a joke that did the rounds in Leningrad in the 1930s, the time of the Great Terror. Question: What's the tallest building in the city? Answer: 'The "Big Building" on Liteiny Prospekt (the local NKVD headquarters), because from there you can see Kolyma.'[2] It seemed to me now that they had brought Kolyma to the walls of the Kremlin. 'Well, what do you think of it?' I asked my friend from London. He shrugged his shoulders and said, 'It looks like an identity crisis.'

A Colonial Landscape

In the mid seventeenth century, in the reign of Tsar Aleksei Mikhailovich, an elephant appeared in the moat by the Kremlin, which had been dug out along Red Square but was almost never filled with water. The elephant was a present from the Shah of Persia, Abbas II. It did not last very long. Once the weather turned cold, as it says in the chronicles of the time, 'the elephant expired'. The Zaryadye Park is just like the elephant: a whim of the Sovereign, a royal gift. It is made up of far-away landscapes, imported plants and borrowed meanings imposed on this place. It is a clone of global architecture, of the High Line Park in New York City – the project of Zaryadye was created by the Diller Scofidio + Renfro bureau that designed a park on an abandoned railway line in Manhattan.

The problem with Zaryadye is that it is a project that does not match its context or its environment; it is what designers and architects would call 'anti-environmental'. It follows in the outdated modernist concept of 'panopticon' and attraction, the colonial idea of the appropriation of space. It was born out of the context of 'internal colonialism' and 'the mastery of nature', whereby a notable space is taken over in the very heart of the city and an object is placed there that is fantastic and alien – all for the glory of the rulers and for the public's amusement.

Yet a thousand ideas were buried inside Zaryadye, from the archaeological (this was an ancient market district, with Chinese, Jewish, Tatar and German quarters, with a Protestant church and two synagogues, with the Velikaya (Great) Street that in past centuries led down to the piers of the full-flowing Moskva River) to the ecological; it would have been more worthwhile to create a classic Moscow garden with native trees: lindens, oaks, lilac bushes, making shady alleys . . . Instead, the colonial concept was chosen, to reproduce different Eurasian climatic regions (from the steppe to the bog and the tundra) to show them with an imperial splendour, like in the Soviet patriotic song: 'Wide is my Motherland!'

It is the imperial idea that dominates the park, crushing the spirit of the place: the Moscow antiquity and the natural landscapes of central Russia. And it is this inability to preserve, to draw out and to promote Russia's own indigenous ideas, making do instead with the 'star dust' of world architecture, that shows an inescapable provinciality, the Russian cargo-cult. Russia is global only when it produces its own unique cultural forms (like, for example, the Russian icon or the Russian avant-garde, which grew out of lubok, the Russian popular print);

yet it is provincial when it simply imports foreign ideas, and Zaryadye is a typical example of such provincialism.

Nostalgia for the Empire

We decided to have supper in the 'gastro-centre' in the heart of the park. We gave the 'Voskhod' restaurant a miss – named in honour of the rocket that took Yury Gagarin into space – with its heavy Soviet design, where behind the windows red-faced men in white shirts had taken off their jackets and were eating steak and drinking wine from enormous wine-glasses, under the gaze of a bored waiter; and so we went into the food court next door. This was a postmodern space that looked as if it had been decorated by Terry Gilliam, dominated by colonial kitsch. Tropical creepers hung from the ceiling; *plov* [a Central Asian dish, similar to pilaf – Tr.] was being tossed around in a cauldron in one corner; in another, lobster claws lay on a bed of ice; and a little farther away, next to a samovar, a peddler wearing an untucked Russian shirt was selling *baranki* and *kalachi*, traditional Russian bagels and buns.

We sat down underneath a huge mincing-machine the size of a two-storey house at a table that, apparently, was also supposed to represent the tundra – in the countertop under the glass there was a bunch of mosses, with bugs and worms crawling around within them. We ordered dishes from various peoples of the USSR: *pel'meny* (dumplings) from the Urals, and *pirogi* (pies) from Ossetia, washed down with wine from the Taman Peninsula, cider from St Petersburg, and *samogon* (home-made strong liquor). Plastic boards hung from the ceiling bearing the names of dozens of Soviet cities: Tula, Grozny, Minsk, Karaganda. Excited guests were taking selfies with the names of their hometowns.

And it was there, in the restaurant, that I finally understood that Zaryadye is a space for imperial nostalgia, a wake for a lost country that is being reconstituted in this gastronomic mish-mash. The Zaryadye project is essentially colonial, it exoticizes the Russian space, its nature and its scenery, its cuisine and its specialities, bizarrely mixing the global and the provincial, international architecture with Soviet aesthetics. And, in this sense, it really does demonstrate a crisis of identity, that very sense of loss and emptiness in which we now live: the designers of the park have inadvertently made an exact model of our times.

Memorial to Russian Resentment

Over the course of a few years, I grew used to him and even felt a sense of sympathy. No longer young and a little overweight, the guy stands on a little island in the middle of the Garden Ring Road, separated from people by the endless streams of traffic, and rather lost against the background of the gloomy Sberbank skyscraper, which reminds one of the towers of Mordor in *The Lord of the Rings*. He holds in his hands an automatic rifle, but awkwardly, as if wanting to push it away from himself; he is like a peasant who has heard a noise in the garden, and gone out onto the porch at night with his gun and is standing there, cautiously looking around. Behind him they have hoisted a huge globe made of granite; a representation of planet Earth, above which, like a trademark, there's the image of a Kalashnikov rifle. At the base of the memorial, a lonely bouquet of carnations is wilting. People do not often go up to this memorial, and it has about it an air of melancholy, of solitude and of death.

Russia is experiencing a 'memorial era': wars for memory and battles for memorials take the place of elections and politics; the public argues over the statue of Prince Vladimir,[1] or Ivan the Terrible, or the bust of Stalin in the Alley of Leaders in Moscow. But even against a background of the complete memorialization of Russian rulers and military leaders, the monument to Mikhail Kalashnikov stands out. It looks awkward and does not really belong on the Garden Ring; yet at the same time, it suits the spirit of the age. It is not a memorial to a person, but to a rifle, and is possibly the main memorial of the past decade in modern Russia. In the thirty years of its post-Soviet transition, Russia has come full circle: after passing through the temptations of globalization, democracy and the market, the nation has returned to an idea as simple as the click of a gun: to the formula of 'Kalashnikov'.

Its basic idea is a primitive one. Like all the main Russian symbols – vodka, matryoshka dolls and fur hats with ear-flaps – the Kalashnikov is simple and unpretentious. And, like each of them, it was not invented by Russians. Vodka, *aqua vitae*, was brought to Russia by Genoese traders in the fourteenth century. The matryoshka doll, which Russia presented at the World Expo in Paris in 1900, is actually of Japanese origin. The Russian version was a modified figure of the Japanese god of wealth, Fukurokuju, adopted by Russian folk art in the last decade of the nineteenth century. And the fur hat is a hybrid of the 'Malakhai' hat worn by the Golden Horde and the Norwegian 'Nansen's hat'.

Similarly, the Kalashnikov was actually stolen from the Germans. In 1946, the legendary German gunsmith Hugo Schmeisser, the inventor of the Sturmgewehr StG-44 assault rifle, was forcibly taken to the USSR from Thuringia together with a large group of designers, and it is the Sturmgewehr StG-44 that was the basis for the new Soviet weapon. In 1947–8, the German weapon was re-worked by the savvy engineer Sergeant Mikhail Kalashnikov, to make it simpler and cheaper. Kalashnikov was from a peasant background and known for his native wit and ability to economize (as the seventeenth child in a family of nineteen children – although only eight of them survived – he knew all about economizing), and what he came up with became the legendary Soviet AK-47.

As a result, the basic and trouble-free assault rifle was born, which was incredibly cheap, and made of stamped steel and plywood, a symbol of the soldier's ingenuity and Russian cunning, which can defeat the enemy's sophisticated technology. You can open a tin of meat with the body of the gun, dig a trench with the butt and use it as a paddle in water; you can shoot it even when it's covered in sand, and you don't have to clean it particularly carefully. The French magazine *Libération* named the AK the greatest invention of the twentieth century, outstripping both nuclear weapons and Space technology. And the AK came fourth in *Playboy* magazine's list of 'Fifty Things That Changed the World', beaten only by the Apple Macintosh computer, the contraceptive pill and the Sony video recorder.

But consider the differences: the first three inventions freed people's imagination and creativity. The computer and the video recorder led to the information revolution, by making data personal and accessible from home. The contraceptive pill led to a sexual revolution, separating reproduction and pleasure in sex, and freeing women from being just machines for bearing children. But once it became the single most widespread example of small arms in the world (accounting for 15 per cent of the market), the Kalashnikov rifle brought about a revolution of a different type: an explosion in the growth of the 'markets of violence' and of low-intensity conflicts. Kalashnikovs are riveted on someone's knee in a home workshop in Herat in Afghanistan or Peshawar in Pakistan; the Yugoslav composer Goran Bregović wrote a song about it; it is the weapon of choice for Colombian narco-barons and Somali pirates; the firstborn in peasant families in countries in Central Africa are called 'Kalash'; the AK appears on the crests of Zimbabwe and East Timor, and on the flag of Mozambique.

In Russia itself, the AK is a cult item. Films, books and history lessons are devoted to it. For decades, Mikhail Kalashnikov himself was a national icon, an honoured guest at presidiums and state functions, a lieutenant-general and a lifelong member of the Soviet parliament, the Supreme Soviet. His rifle was an essential part of the Soviet person's everyday life: we studied it in basic military training classes in school, starting from the fifth or sixth grade, when we were 12 or 13 years old, and every single school had a couple of training rifles. Targets were set for the time it would take to strip down and reassemble the rifle: to pass the test, a schoolchild had to be able to put it together in one minute, at the same time accurately naming each component. To this day I can remember the words 'hand-guard' and 'sear', but I have forgotten long ago what they mean. During the two years of military service that most of the male population of Russia went through, the Kalashnikov became a man's main companion. To this day, it is an important part of the symbolism of Russian life: you see the profile of the Kalashnikov on bumper stickers on cars; people use it as their avatar on social media; and it is tattooed on shoulders. Patriotic propaganda proudly talks about it as Russia's contribution to world civilization (more than 100 million examples of it have been sold), and at the memorial's opening ceremony the then minister of culture, Vladimir Medinsky, called it 'Russia's cultural brand'. As the writer Viktor Yerofeyev noted, 'this would be like the French describing the guillotine as "the national educator of feelings"'.[2]

In this sense, the Kalashnikov is Russia's answer to the global world. A quarter of a century ago, Russia tried to join that world. It opened its borders, it acquired knowledge, it was integrated into global institutions, even toying with the idea of joining the European Union or NATO. But in the first decade of this century, movement in this direction ceased, and in 2014, with the annexation of Crimea and the occupation of the Donbas, it turned decisively in the opposite direction. The country could not cope with the complexity of the modern world, leaving behind the Skolkovo techno-park, with its pretensions to be a Russian Silicone Valley, as well as the Higher School of Economics, a modern university that wanted to enter the list of the top 100 universities in the world, and the plans for the Russian smartphone and for the Russian electric car. Russia waved goodbye to all this and returned to its basic pattern of centuries past: mobilization, war – and the Kalashnikov rifle.

The memorial on the Garden Ring is just a tombstone to yet another unsuccessful attempt to modernize Russia, the jealousy of a pupil who has not been recognized; it is a symbol of provinciality and peripherality, of yet another country that has not caught up with globalization. It is a memorial to Russian resentment, which is now coming back at the world in the most unexpected and terrifying manner.

Thus Spake Zhirinovsky

The patriarch of Russian politics, Vladimir Zhirinovsky, died. At just 75 years of age, he certainly was not the oldest – on the Russian Olympus, this is just the age of maturity – and far from the most titled, but he was definitely one of the pillars of the post-Soviet era. What's more, it was Zhirinovsky who, in a clownish and grotesque manner, formed the political programme of revanchism that was adopted as the official doctrine of Russia in the 2020s; and he became the godfather of Russian fascism, which grew to its full height with the start of the war in Ukraine.

The holding of his funeral service in the Cathedral of Christ the Saviour and the presence of President Putin (or else someone who looked very much like him) finally canonized the dear departed as the key politician of the past thirty years. Many years before his death, he had predicted how his own funeral would be, just as he had predicted many other things, including the start of the war in Ukraine (he was out by just two days). This gift for prophecy speaks not only about how well informed he was, but also about how correctly he felt the *Zeitgeist*, the spirit of the time – and formulated this spirit himself.

He started out as the spoiler of the democratic movement. He was allegedly sent to the opposition by the KGB in the guise of the leader of the first social-democratic, then liberal-democratic, party. As a politician with a dictatorial bent, it was predictable that he and democracy would not get along, and with his unique perception he found the exact topic that would lead to his triumph and, as a result, to Russia's demise. In Russia's first ever presidential elections in 1991, he unexpectedly announced that he would put 'the Russian question at the very point of the needle': '155 million Russians are in the most downtrodden and insulted position! No nation has been so badly smeared!' This was how his star began to rise. He came third in those elections with nearly 8 per cent of the vote, and in the parliamentary elections in 1993 his Liberal-Democratic Party of Russia (LDPR) won, having gained 23 per cent of votes cast, which elicited from the liberal publicist, the then master of minds and former MP Yuri Karyakin, an epic exclamation: 'Russia, come to your senses, you've gone crazy!'

The heralds of perestroika ignored the existence of that same 'crazy' Russia that became Zhirinovsky's electoral estate and that today is shooting, torturing, raping and looting in Bucha, Hostomel and Mariupol. At the heart of these voters were men of middle age and older, those who lived in the suburbs, in depressed regions, in small towns, poorly educated and with low social capital, and with a military or criminal background: in other words, those who lost most from the reforms, who felt insulted by the world of freedom and globalization and were nostalgic for the Soviet past. They were not the dominant force in Russia, neither electorally nor demographically, but they represented that social heartland, 'the blokes in the garages',[1] that the Kremlin ideologue Vladislav Surkov was later to call 'the deep nation' (*glubinny narod*). Zhirinovsky began to speak the language of these people, opening up their problems, giving them a voice and a vote, legitimizing their grudges against life and turning it into his political capital. He was far from the intellectual shambles of Russian nationalism, with Dostoevsky in its hand and cabbage in its beard, and also from the gloomy determination, shaved heads and flattened knuckles of the neo-Nazis who took part in the 'Russian marches' (regular events organized by Russian nationalists and fascists), but he had the gift of speaking from his platforms about things that were considered taboo, indecent, marginal, that were only talked about in the kitchens, the beer bars and in those same garages. Thanks to him, these subjects came into public speech and the language of politics and, as a result, became a part of the discourse of power.

The Four Horsemen of the Apocalypse

Zhirinovsky legitimized the four main elements of Russian fascism, the principal one being the idea of offence, on which the difficult moral complex of resentment is based. Nietzsche called resentment 'the moral of slaves', the envy of the loser, the helpless hatred of the slave towards his master, whom he considers to be the root cause of all his misfortune. Zhirinovsky talked about offence before it became politically fashionable. Furthermore, at the start of the 1990s, the political and economic elite were in a state of ecstasy about the possibilities that were opening up, and about the plasticity of reality and the ability to change everything in an instant. Yes, there were seizures of property by 'raiding' [scams that led to businesses being illegally taken over, often by gangs – Tr.], bankruptcies, people eking out a semi-starving existence, street crime and ethnic conflicts on the country's fringes; but mostly the Soviet past and the rotten system were blamed for all this, and the West was seen as the example and the civilization of the future. In those days, a large part of the population did not feel offended by the outside world, and were more likely to want to join it.

Zhirinovsky was the first to speak publicly about Russia being offended and humiliated. I remember my surprise the first time I saw in Moscow a huge election poster for the LDPR on a billboard that proclaimed, 'For Russians, for the Poor!' At the time, I thought: 'Why are Russians poor?' Compared to Central Asia, Moldova, Belarus and Ukraine, Russia in the mid-2000s looked like an island of prosperity. It was attracting investment, building its clumsy capitalism and accepting migrants. However, Zhirinovsky cleverly played on the narrative of the post-Soviet losers, and by the middle of the first decade of the twenty-first century all the political elite were talking about how Russia had been offended. It was at this point, in 2005, that Putin started to bemoan the collapse of the USSR as the 'greatest geopolitical catastrophe of the twentieth century'.

Out of this feeling of being offended grew the second element of Zhirinovsky's fascist clowning: revenge for the Empire. His election slogan from 1993, 'I Will Raise Russia Up from Its Knees!' had predated by a good fifteen years what was to become one of Vladimir Putin's favourite slogans. The idea of the reconstitution of the USSR runs like a red thread through his speeches: 'Our wish to all the former Soviet republics: you have wandered around, but that's enough. It's time to come home.' Twenty years later, these outrageous statements seriously came home to roost in Putin's declarations about 'presents from the Russian people' given to the republics of the Soviet Union, which would have to be given back.

The third horseman of Zhirinovsky's Apocalypse was expansionism. One of his most famous sayings, about the Russian soldier washing his boots in the Indian Ocean, may have been apocryphal (our hero rather listlessly denied it) – but whether or not he said it, he certainly dreamt about *The Final Charge to the South* (the title of his book), and called for the bombing of Baghdad, Tbilisi and Istanbul, thus realizing the long-held Russian imperial dream of 'hanging your shield on the gates of Tsargrad'.[2] And here, too, we can see how Putin followed Zhirinovsky's thoughts about Russia looking southwards in his foreign policy: the war in Syria in 2015, constant tension in relations with Turkey, and Russian armed involvement in Libya and the Central African Republic.

Finally, the fourth element: xenophobia. Zhirinovsky hated everyone: from the people of the Caucasus, which he promised to fence in with barbed wire, to Ukraine, which he did not consider to be a state, calling for Russia to seize Sevastopol way back in 1990; from immigrants to Jews, whom he accused of stirring up anti-Semitism. He could not stand liberals, multiculturalism or the tolerance of the West, all of which was strange to hear from someone who was an extravert and a comedian, half-Jewish by blood, and bisexual – someone who had a particular liking for red and canary yellow jackets, and whose retinue was invariably full of handsome young men. He could have been the ideal object of hatred for those very same 'blokes in the garages', but instead he helped them formulate their views rejecting everything new, garish and foreign.

None of this fitted in with the tolerant and pluralistic atmosphere of the 1990s; but it quickly came into the mainstream with the rapidly growing archaism of the Putin era, with its chauvinism, militarism, Orthodoxy, traditionalist 'bonds' (*skrepy*) and homophobia. The cultivation of hatred for 'the Other' became the basis of domestic policy and of the new social contract. In Putin's third term, after the breaking-up of the protest movement on Bolotnaya Square in 2012, it became the key technology of power, leading to the final formation of fascism in Russia. Over the past ten years, various actors have taken on the role of 'the Other': foreign adopters of Russian children; LGBT people; feminists; liberals; 'the fifth column'; the falsifiers of history; 'our Western partners', as Russian leaders sarcastically call the West; America and 'the Anglo-Saxons' (a word that has suddenly appeared in the lexicon of Russian propaganda, as if it has come straight from the pages of Hitler's press); the innocuous Czech Republic, which has unexpectedly emerged on the list of Russia's greatest enemies; and proud Poland, stuck there like a bone in the throat of the curators of Russia's 'history policy'. And finally, exactly as Zhirinovsky predicted, Ukraine has become enemy number one.

No doubt historians of the future will work out how and when Ukraine took hold of Putin's paranoid imagination. Did it happen in 2004, at the time of the first Maidan Revolution,[3] when 'colour revolutions' flared up around the perimeter of the Empire? Or was it at the time of the second Maidan, in 2013? Or was it due to some unknown childhood trauma? Or the adult jealousy of a rejected and despised husband? Whatever it was, the fact is that, for Putin, Ukrainians became the same as the Jews were for Hitler: a thorn in his vision of the universe. All his pseudo-historical essays of the previous year, all his bitter comments, his seething contempt and hatred for Ukraine, bear witness to the fact that he had decided 'finally to settle the Ukrainian question'. In his extermination of Ukraine, which is taking place before our very eyes, Putin is following the behests of his spiritual father, Zhirinovsky, who easily threw nuclear bombs in his incendiary speeches.

Beware the Postmodern!

Now we come to the main question: how was it that Russia, with its progressive urban class, its developed public sphere, which had for a long time had free media, with its acute awareness of the value of the spoken word – how was it that, over the course of thirty years, we witnessed the birth, the formation and the institutionalization of genuine, textbook, fascism? Why was Zhirinovsky's xenophobic invective simply treated as a bit of a laugh, and not a crime for which he should have been held accountable?

It seems that the answer lies in the fact that the new Russian authoritarianism, and the fascist regime which followed, came from the womb of the postmodernism of the 1990s. Caught up in the cultural context of the *fin de siècle*, with the effortless fall of the Berlin Wall and then of the Soviet 'Empire of Evil' (both, it turned out, were made of cardboard); with its 'end of history' and 'world without borders'; with the quotations from Jacques Derrida ('There is nothing outside the text') and Jean Baudrillard ('The Gulf War did not take place'); with the novels of the leading postmodern Russian writers, Vladimir Sorokin and Viktor Pelevin – with all this, Russian politics was shaped as a game, a fictitious script.

Against this background, Vladimir Zhirinovsky's political theatre became possible. The enlightened part of society regarded him with a mixture of horror and delight, rather like the novels of the Marquis de Sade, with their edifying tortures; the plays of Antonin Artaud's 'Theatre of Cruelty'; or the physiological stories by Jean Genet – all of which were published in Russia at that time. Many people liked the way Zhirinovsky fluidly crossed borders, how he deftly worked with forbidden subjects and how he could aestheticize violence. Here we can talk about the destructive role played by the provincially, enthusiastically accepted, postmodern in the unprepared consciousness of Russia. He justified the forbidden (the base instincts of the crowd), he smeared moral judgements (it is ridiculous to talk about ethics if all around is just a game), he brought onto the political stage the most grotesque forms of neo-conservatism and neo-Stalinism: from Alexander Dugin and Alexander Prokhanov to Eduard Limonov and Vladimir Zhirinovsky – they all danced at Satan's postmodern ball![4]

On the other hand, Zhirinovsky's buffoonery was in demand by the *siloviki* and, ever increasingly, by the Kremlin. They saw this as a useful way to drain resentment, right-wing radicalism and proto-fascism, which were marginalized in Zhirinovsky's travelling circus: he loved to tour the country by train, attracting crowds of people in cities and towns; in the capital, he enjoyed declaiming by the Sokolniki metro station, where, in the manner of Fidel Castro, he would deliver hours-long monologues about the international situation. He would get his 10 to 15 per cent in the electoral niche that the LDPR had created, although this steadily declined as the years passed – the 23 per cent that he took in the 1993 parliamentary elections remained the high point of his success.

At the same time, the *siloviki* unleashed the hunt for anyone in this sector – Russian nationalists and right-wing radicals – who was ready to start genuine political action. While Zhirinovsky was amusing the crowds with his escapades, the FSB and the Interior Ministry (which created a special centre, 'E', to fight extremism) cleared out the whole right wing of the political spectrum, then went after other political activists. After the breaking-up of the Bolotnaya Square protests, they turned their attention to 'working' decisively with the liberals, 'the angry urban class' and the zones of civic mobilization. In their pursuit of radicals, genuine and imaginary, the *siloviki* created a different type of radicalism, to which more, and more frightening, resources were devoted: the state terror machinery, which can do nothing but fight against others – gays, liberals, Islamists, Jehovah's Witnesses[5] – seeing all of them as their daily bread. Fascism developed exactly where it was least expected. A new type had entered the scorched political arena: an Orthodox Chekist, carrying a book by Ivan Ilyin.[6] A radically different political era had begun – and it is the one we are living in now.

A New Frankenstein

In the end, Zhirinovsky's clown-like fascism, which was created by the security services and fed by the Kremlin, unchecked neither by civil society nor by the political or judicial system, became a routine part of the country's politics, turned into a discourse of power and was supported by the repressive state machinery. The ideas of imperial revenge were attached to the police apparatus and Russia's military power that had been increasing over the past twenty years, and this produced a Frankenstein's monster: state fascism. This is exactly the 'new fascism' about which the American philosopher Judith Butler writes. It contains, firstly, legalized 'freedom to hate', and, secondly, it mobilizes resentment to awaken in people a feeling of wounded national greatness. Today, the official propaganda mouthpieces trumpet Zhirinovsky's old ideas, but now use them to justify the killing of Ukrainians. The raving fantasies of an eccentric politician – about global revenge, the recreation of the USSR and the destruction of Ukraine – have gone from mere fiction, rhetorical figures and political technologies to being the Iskander and Tochka missiles and the cluster bombs that today are raining down on Ukrainian cities.

The politician himself did not live to see the triumph of his fantasies. At the start of February 2022, he fell ill with coronavirus, on top of which he had pneumonia, and he was put on a ventilator. Just after the start of the war, on 26 February, he was put into an artificial coma. His later biological existence was surrounded by guesswork and rumour. Some say that he came round, read the news and even 'worked on documents'. Others assert that he did not come out of the coma and died on 25 March. His body was then kept in the mortuary for two weeks so that Putin could say his farewells; after all, no one, alive or dead, was allowed to come close to the sovereign without observing the fourteen-day quarantine. The inconsistency of these conspiracy theories was appropriate for the comic figure of the deceased; as Mark Twain joked, 'The reports of my death are greatly exaggerated'.

Vladimir Putin's personally demonstrative and intimate farewell to Zhirinovsky – even the honour guard was removed from the hall – once again underlined the unique role that the deceased played in the life of the president. The last time that Putin had bid someone farewell with such feeling was when he attended the funeral of his first judo trainer, Anatoly Rakhlin, in St Petersburg in August 2013. We thought that Zhirinovsky was simply the tsar's favourite court jester; but it turned out that he was his mentor. The body of the LDPR leader was decontaminated and buried in the Novodevichy Cemetery; but the virus of fascism and Zhirinovsky's work live on. Indeed, today we are living in the post-apocalyptic world dreamt up by Vladimir Zhirinovsky.

The Offering Made to the Ninth of May

The Fear of Holidays

I suddenly realized that I have an eerie feeling: for ten years now, I have been afraid of Russian state holidays, knowing that, each time, the authorities will celebrate them with some new bout of repressions. Most of all, I am afraid of elections and referenda. It is already the third time that the election cycle has been preceded by a stronger persecution of the media, observers, opposition candidates and activists – on top of the habitual falsification of results, they have added repression, to have the elections under complete control. New Year is also a dangerous time. During the fuss in the build-up to the holiday, and before everyone goes off for their New Year break, the State Duma, giving no time for protest, usually passes in packages the most odious laws, such as, for example, the 'Dima Yakovlev Law' of 28 December 2012, which forbade foreigners from adopting Russian orphans.

In a time of war, holidays take on a particularly sinister feel. In 2022, I had an especially unpleasant premonition in the lead-up to 23 February, the Day of the Defenders of the Fatherland (or Red Army Day as it was called in Soviet times, celebrated since 1918). I feared that this would be the day that Russia would begin its attack on Ukraine, thus turning the Day of the Defenders of the Fatherland into the Day of the Aggressors. I was just one day out. The war began in the early morning of 24 February. I was wary on 12 April, fearing that Russia would mark Cosmonauts' Day (the anniversary of Yury Gagarin's first Space flight on this day in 1961) with a volley of Grad, Tochka and Iskander missiles against Ukrainian cities. Then it was with awful trepidation that I awaited 9 May, guessing that Putin would want to create a parade on this day to celebrate Victory over imaginary Ukrainian Nazism; maybe he would even force Ukrainian soldiers who had been taken prisoner to march across Red Square. This is what they did in Donetsk in August 2014, holding a procession of Ukrainian prisoners of war, then sending a water truck behind them to wash away all trace of them – exactly as they did with the procession of captured German prisoners in Moscow in July 1944.[1]

In Putin's Russia, Victory Day has gone through a mind-blowing evolution. At the start of the century, it was still regarded as 'the holiday with tears in our eyes' (in the words of the Soviet patriotic song 'Victory Day'); but then it began to turn into a military-patriotic show, especially at the start of the 2000s when the Ribbon of St George appeared and began to be displayed everywhere.[2] By 2010 it had become a massive symbolic machine. Putin's state had found its point of reference in the Ninth of May, the myth of its founding. It was born not in 1917 with the October Revolution; not in 1991, when the Soviet Union collapsed; not even in 1999, the year that Putin came to power; but in 1945, at the peak of the might of Stalin's USSR, when a 15-million-strong Red Army stood in the centre of Europe and Stalin divided up the world with the victorious nations. Putin probably imagines himself as the Generalissimo in a white military tunic with a pipe in his hand standing over the map of Europe at Yalta in 1945, or as Tsar Alexander I in a sleek uniform at the Vienna Congress of 1815, surrounded by the rulers of Europe and waltzing couples; whereas, in fact, he looks more like the Great Dictator in Charlie Chaplin's film of that name, in the scene where a daydreaming dictator takes the globe off its stand and starts to spin it round on his finger.

The Ninth of May now fills all historical time for Russia; it has turned into both a memorial cult and a guide to action. In the middle of the first decade of this century, vainglorious stickers started to appear on cars, bearing the words '1941–1945. We Can Repeat It!', adorned with obscene pictures of how the hammer-and-sickle is raping the swastika. (Is it worth noting how this cult of rape turned out in the Ukrainian towns of Bucha and Irpen?) Victory Day has become the optic through which Russia sees the world, using it to show all the offence it feels, all its complexes, its aggression and its resentment. The holiday has been turned into an endless liturgy, an ecstatic reliving of the past, which has taken the place of people's unhappy everyday life.

The Cult of the Dead

Over the last twenty years, the Ninth of May has become a religious cult. Towering over this whole symbolical universe is the monstrous Cathedral of Victory in the 'Patriot' military park outside Moscow, which looks like something drawn with illustrations from *Star Wars* or Gothic comics – brooding, threatening, standing in an empty field between ominously symmetrical lawns. While trying to depict the idea of permanent war, this sanctuary of militarism simply turns into pathos, comedy and kitsch. The marches of 'the Immortal Regiment' take place in honour of the cult of Victory and remind one of religious processions, only with portraits of heroes of the Great Patriotic War in place of icons. It started out as a citizens' initiative by the television channel TV2 in the Siberian city of Tomsk, but the ritual was quickly picked up by the state and turned into a bureaucratic act, with state employees forced to take part, carrying generic portraits of unknown war heroes. Indeed, it is not just about the War: Stalinists drag along portraits of their moustachioed idol, and at one procession Natalya Poklonskaya, who was the Crimean prosecutor after it was annexed by Russia, walked along with an icon of Tsar Nicholas II.

The portraits do, indeed, acquire the attributes of icons, as for example in a propaganda cartoon made by the movement against abortion. In it, a girl tells her boyfriend on the telephone that she is pregnant; he suggests that she has an abortion. The girl ponders on this and, at that moment, exactly like in the hagiographic genre of 'the talking icon', an army nurse in a portrait from 'the Immortal Regiment' that is hanging on the wall starts speaking to her: 'Don't have an abortion! You'll have a son, he'll be a soldier!' The father then disappears from the scene, the girl gives birth, becomes a single parent, and a few years later is seen going off to the Victory parade with her son.

The mythology of Victory does not always match up with reality and calls for blind faith. What happened with the so-called '28 Panfilovite Heroes' is a case in point. Fighters of the Ivan Panfilov Rifle Division allegedly stopped a division of German tanks at the Dubosekovo Halt during the Battle for Moscow in December 1941, thus becoming the principal martyrs in the Soviet cult of war heroes. However, research by the military procurator's office in November 1947 revealed that one of the heroes who 'perished' actually surrendered in the spring of 1942 and then served in the German army. It turned out that the whole story had been made up by a correspondent for the army newspaper *Krasnaya Zvezda* ['Red Star'] in January 1942, loosely basing this beautiful legend on actual battles that had taken place in the area. The myth took on its own life, became a part of the Soviet patriotic canon, and streets and schools were named after the heroes, and memorials raised to them. And when the director of the Russian State Archive, Sergei Mironenko, revealed that this old story was false, he was accused of insulting their memory. The then minister of culture, Vladimir Medinsky, replied that a myth that had inspired generations of Soviet people was more important than the historical facts. Shortly after this, Mironenko was relieved of his post.

This cult has spread among the masses and become overwhelmed with rituals that some scornfully call *pobedobesie*: 'Victory frenzy'. People decorate anything that comes to hand with the ribbon of St George, the symbol of the Victory, from bottles of vodka at the celebratory meal, to the dog's collar; they tie them in their hair and wear them in place of a tie; they decorate their cars with military slogans such as 'To Berlin!', 'War Trophy from Germany' or 'For the Motherland, for Stalin!' What has become especially popular is dressing children up in mock uniforms – even small babies. They put on little imitation soldiers' tunics, caps and boots; they are presented with toy guns; their strollers and cots are painted to look like tanks and other military vehicles. Children play a particular role here, giving everything a higher moral sanction for sacrifice and heroism. It inscribes the cult of the Victory into the ritual cycles of spring, like the appearance of young shoots on dead, scorched earth. In another advertisement for the anti-abortion movement, one part of the poster shows a human embryo saying from its mother's womb, 'Defend me today and I'll defend you tomorrow'; then, elsewhere on the poster, he has grown into a boy wearing an oversize army helmet and holding a Kalashnikov rifle.

Celebrating War

From an object of collective memory (including family, local and private memories), from the living history of the nation,

Victory was turned into an indisputable moral absolute, in which no criticism is possible of the Soviet Union ('the Victorious Nation') or of Stalin; in which the right of force has been legitimized, and the sense of isolation – 'we stand alone against the world' – has been formed. Ethics are turned into laws, and new legal norms are accepted in the name of the Victory. A whole series of amendments have been introduced regulating historical memory, with legislative prohibitions on 'likening the Soviet Union to Nazi Germany', 'denial of the USSR's decisive role in the Victory' and 'the contestation of the results of the Second World War'; these are now considered criminal offences. Repressions are carried out in the name of the Victory: in 2021, Alexei Navalny was sentenced on made-up charges of 'insulting war veterans'. Foreign policy démarches are carried out in the name of the Victory: think of Russia's diplomatic wars with Poland and the Czech Republic about Second World War memorials, and the infuriated historical essays by Putin attacking the countries of Eastern Europe. And now, in the name of the Victory, Russia has unleashed an aggressive, land-grabbing war.

This is the principal, and frightening, result of the militaristic cult of the Ninth of May. Instead of honouring the Victory as the end of war (Evgeniy Vuchetic's sculpture *Let Us Beat Swords into Ploughshares*, which stands outside the UN headquarters in New York City, is an example of this), instead of celebrating peace, Russia now celebrates war itself. Instead of the mantra 'May there never be a war', which all the post-War Soviet generations repeated, Russia has now come up with the revanchist slogan, 'We Can Repeat It!'

And this is exactly what happened on 24 February 2022. Under the invented excuse of 'de-nazifying' Ukraine, taken from propaganda clichés, Russia unleashed the biggest war in Europe since the Second World War. But, having decided to repeat 1945, Russia made a mistake with its role in this bloody historical reconstruction. Ironically, it is now playing the part not of the liberating Soviet warriors, but of the German invaders. History has come full circle and closed in on itself: those who defeated the Nazis have become a pathetic copy of them. Today, the true successors of 1941 to 1945 are not the Russian occupiers who have invaded a neighbouring country, but the Ukrainians, defending their own Motherland.

. . . At the height of the pandemic and lockdowns in 2020, the Kremlin's grand celebration of the seventy-fifth anniversary of the Victory was disrupted. This was meant to be the culmination of a months-long propaganda campaign. It was decided to compensate for the failure of this enormous event by holding a massive firework display all over Moscow, but the organizers clearly overdid it with the amount of gunpowder and arranged a real bombardment. I watched the event from the top floor of an apartment block on Moscow's western fringe: separate volleys at different points of the city merged into a constant fiery mess, Moscow was covered in smoke from the bloody bursts of flame; it was like the Great Fire of Moscow in 1812, when the locals set the entire city on fire before surrendering it to Napoleon. On the outskirts of the park next to my apartment block, spectators hoarsely shouted 'Hooray!' On the Zhivopisny Bridge, a long overpass over the floodplain of the Moskva River, dozens of cars stopped, their hazard lights flashing, and people got out to watch this fiery extravaganza. At that point I remembered the words of the Russian poet Alexander Blok, during the Revolution of 1917, 'We'll set the world aflame in blood',[3] and it struck me for the first time that, for the sake of its Victory Day, Russia was capable of destroying the world.

The firework display ended, people left the park and the cars drove away. But the nauseating small of gunpowder hung in the air all night. Later it rained, and by morning the air was clear once more.

A Long Farewell to Empire

The Half-Life of the USSR

It was a true Russian winter that set in early in 1991, frosty and snowy. At 7.35 on the cold evening of 25 December, as the year was fading away, the red flag of the Soviet Union, lit up by spotlights, was lowered from the dome of the principal building in the Kremlin, and in its place was raised the white, blue and red tricolour of Russia. The USSR collapsed in an insultingly simple fashion, unnoticed, as if it were an everyday occurrence. It seemed to repeat the inglorious end of the Russian Empire in the way that it was described by the philosopher Vasily Rozanov, in his diary *The Apocalypse of Our Time*, which was published shortly after the 1917 Revolution:

> Russia faded away in two days. Three at the most. They couldn't even shut down the *New Times*[1] newspaper as quickly as Russia shut down. It was amazing to see how it all simply crumbled away, to the little details, to the particulars. In reality, there had never been such a shock, not even the 'Great Migration Period'.[2]

History repeated itself seventy-four years later, in 1991. Even
the Communist Party newspaper, *Pravda*, could not have been
shut down as quickly as the Soviet Union shut down, a fake
empire made of cardboard and not at all scary on that frozen
December evening. The USSR split into fourteen independent
states that were viable in varying degrees, and one imaginary
power, which had ceased to be an empire but had not become
a nation. Russia became the legal successor to the Soviet Union
and inherited not only its nuclear arsenal and its place on the
United Nations Security Council, but also its pretence of being
an empire, its spatial scope, its geopolitical ambition and its
psychological complexes. In a postcolonial world, at the end of
a century that had witnessed the demise of the main empires
of the modern era – the Ottoman and the Austro-Hungarian
at its start, the Third Reich and the Japanese Empire in the
middle, and the British, French and Dutch Empires in the
second half – there remained a huge Eurasian territory, frozen
in the permafrost of its own past, like a giant fossilized animal.

The short break from empire, marked by Russia's with-
drawal from Central and Eastern Europe and the locations of
geopolitical stand-offs around the world, as well as by a 'parade
of sovereignties' inside the country (following Boris Yeltsin's
famous comment, made in 1990 to representatives of national
autonomies, that they should 'take as much sovereignty as they
are able to swallow'), lasted no more than five years, from 1990
to 1994, and was ended by the first war in Chechnya in 1994–6.
Meanwhile, in the mid-1990s, the initial signs of nostalgia for
the Soviet Union appeared. On New Year's Eve 1995, Russian
TV showed a retro-musical filmed in the style of the Stalin
period, called *Old Songs about the Main Things* (*Stariye pesni o
glavnom*). Leading figures from Russian stage and screen sang
old Soviet songs in the setting of a collective farm of the late
1940s, and it was a triumph. The film was so successful that
new versions of the musical were produced for each of the following four New Year celebrations. The USSR was inexorably

returning as mythology and ideology in the form of Stalin's 'grand style' and tsar-like attitudes in the Kremlin. The ten years of Yeltsin's transition failed to produce for Russia a new style, a new ideology, a new elite or a new nation. The country remained in a dead faint and total uncertainty as regards its identity or its place in the modern world.

Out of this void was born the neo-imperial crusade of Vladimir Putin. As the joke goes, 'the leading politician of the nineteenth century' built his political project on the return of the imperial discourse as the basis for Russian identity. Having no vision for the future, he thrust Russia into history, presenting the country with the illusion of past greatness. The milestones of this imperial renaissance were his speech at the Munich Security Conference in 2007; the war against Georgia in 2008; and in 2014 the annexation of Crimea and the occupation of the Donbas, which brought about a patriotic surge in society known as 'the Crimean euphoria'. The invasion of Ukraine in 2022 became a logical continuation of this neo-imperial trend – characteristically, it used the Soviet slogan of 'de-Nazifying' Ukraine, and Soviet symbols: many Russian tanks were displaying the Soviet red flag and the red star. The Russian authorities in the occupied Ukrainian territories in Kherson and Zaporizhzhia Oblasts were reinstalling statues of Lenin that had been knocked down in accordance with Ukraine's De-Communization Law, and giving back the streets their old Soviet names: Gorky Street, Revolution Street, Proletariat Street. In fact, the USSR turned out to be more significant symbolically than modern Russia.

A State without a Nation

Once again, the Empire in Russia has defeated the nation. It is important to recognize it now, when Russia is suffering a moral, military and, broadly speaking, civilizational defeat in

Ukraine. The attack on Ukraine is a fiasco of the still-born idea of 'the Russian world', *russky mir*,[3] as one lot of Russian speakers bomb, torture and shoot other Russian speakers; as they burn Orthodox churches and demolish the Russian-speaking cities of Mariupol and Kherson. This is not a war for Russia, but for the re-establishment of the Empire, a war of revenge on Ukrainians (it is even crueller, because they are considered 'one of us', 'our brothers') for daring to think that they could break away and follow their own path.

Russia's historical problem is that it is incapable of seeing itself as anything other than an Empire. The pre-revolutionary Russian prime minister Sergei Witte summed it up when he said, 'I do not know what Russia is; I know only the Russian Empire.' In the present century, these words were echoed by the British historian Geoffrey Hosking, when he compared the Russian and British Empires: 'Britain *had* an Empire, while Russia *was* an Empire – and perhaps still is.' And herein lies the main problem: you could remove the overseas colonies from the British (or French, or Belgian, or Dutch, and so on) Empire and the metropolis and the nation state remained. This does not work with Russia, because it colonized itself (what the historian Alexander Etkind described as 'internal colonization'), and you cannot remove the colonies without destroying the whole edifice. Who should be de-colonized: the Far East? Siberia? The Caucasus? Maybe Kaliningrad, the former German city of Königsberg? And what about the internal Turkic and Ugrian colonies along the Volga River? And where will be the Great Russian core – is it Russia to the Ural Mountains, or to the Volga, or just to the Oka, the river that flows to the south of Moscow? And if the Principality of Moscow were to be all that was left, from which century and from which tsar's reign should its boundaries lie?

This is where Putin takes his grievances from when he declares that 'Russia's borders do not end anywhere'; when he writes his verbose essays about the national question, full of poison and resentment in which he criticizes Lenin for the Bolsheviks' nationality policy that promised wide-ranging autonomy to the peoples of the Empire, and denies Ukraine the very right to exist. This is where the feverish ravings of a dying empire come from: the annexation of Crimea; the 'Novorossiya'[4] ('New Russia') project; the dreams of Bessarabia (present-day Moldova), of Northern Kazakhstan, of the Russians in the Baltic States, and even of distant Alaska – Russian land sold to the USA in 1867. As always, the best description of these viral Russian fantasies came from the pen of Nikolai Gogol in the words of the boastful landowner, Nozdryov, in *Dead Souls*: "'This is the boundary,' said Nozdryov. "Everything you see on this side is mine and even on the other side too; all that forest which you see looking blue in the distance and everything beyond it is all mine.'"[5]

A Wounded Tyrannosaurus

Russia does not know its borders and rushes about, shapeless. It lost its Empire, but did not become a nation state, neither of the ethnic Russian nation (the Kremlin strangled Russian nationalism in the bud even before it dealt with the liberals), nor of a civil nation of Russians. On more than one occasion, Russia missed the bus of nation building: in the nineteenth century, when Bismarck brought it to Germany and Garibaldi to Italy; in the middle of the twentieth century, when the largest Western empires crumbled; and at the end of the century, when several territories broke away from the USSR and sailed off on their own, as in the epilogue to Emir Kusturica's film *Underground*, where a separated piece of land floats down the Danube.

Unlike the old metropolis, Ukraine became a nation with its own symbols, with national poet Taras Shevchenko and nationalist icon Stepan Bandera, with its *vyshivanka* shirt,[6] which is so ridiculed in Russia, and that people gladly wear from Lviv to Kharkiv. But this did not happen with Russia: the ethnic nation remained an ethnographic curiosity, rather like the *kokoshnik*[7] that some Russian football fans wore in Moscow during the 2018 football World Cup. What is more, 'Russian' restaurants around the world serve Ukrainian borshch, Caucasian *shashlik* [kebabs], Siberian–Chinese *pelmeny* [meat dumplings] – a mix typical of the cuisine of the Empire. The clumsy attempts to create a nation in Russia in the 1990s were crushed under the boots of the police when they broke up protest meetings, smashed along with opposition politicians and Alexei Navalny's movement, and finally finished off by the war on 24 February 2022.

Russia has still to imagine itself beyond the imperial format; and this is a difficult path for everyone – in Germany and Japan, it ended in national catastrophe; for France, there was the painful setback in its colonial war in Algeria that taught it a good lesson, helping it shake off the imperial delusion. In the same way, Russia must now suffer a painful defeat in Ukraine to rid itself of its imperial ambitions, its great-power arrogance, its 'Big Brother' complex – in fact, of any illusions about brotherhood with anyone – with Ukraine, Belarus or with Russians abroad. It must kill off the Empire within, to build its own nation on civil, human and humane foundations.

. . . In Vladimir Sorokin's anti-utopian novel *Telluria*, which describes Eurasia in the mid twenty-first century, from Madrid to the Altai Mountains, there is a story about a grandmother and her two grandsons who travel into deepest Siberia to pay homage to the statues of 'the three fatal rulers of Russia, the Three Great Bald Ones, who crushed the country of the dragon'. They get off the train at a halt, make their way through the taiga and the bogs by way of secret paths and come upon the cave where the three stone idols stand: 'the first of them, this sly fellow over here with the beard, destroyed the Russian Empire, . . . the second, with glasses and a birthmark on his bald head, tore down the USSR, . . . this third one, with his tiny chin, buried a frightening country that was called the Russian Federation';[8] these were the three great warriors who had destroyed the frightening country in three blows . . . Today we are living through the third act of the collapse of Empire that has been going on for over a hundred years. The first act was in 1917, but was followed by Stalin's restoration of the Empire. The second took place in 1991, followed by Putin's imperial cadenza; and now comes the third, final, act, in which Russia has turned into a parody of itself, giving proof to Hegel's remark that history repeats itself twice: as a tragedy and as a farce.

PART III

THE WAR NATION

The Zombie Apocalypse

A documentary film, *Babiy Yar: The Context*, by the Ukrainian director Sergei Loznitsa, appeared on our screens in 2021. The director showed archive footage of the fascist invasion of Ukraine in the summer of 1941. There were endless columns of tanks bearing the swastika, lorries, motorcycles, artillery pieces, all churning up the dust; and lining the road were gloomy, silent Ukrainian peasants. I have a sense of *déjà vu* when I see pictures of Russia's invasion: lookalike grey columns of military vehicles, dirty, smoky, clumsy, just as if they had come straight out of the 1941 footage; but instead of the swastika on their sides and on their turrets, they have painted the letters 'V' and 'Z'. These columns are phantasmagorical and archaic, as if they were ghosts dug up and crawling off the battlefields of the Second – if not the First – World War, like a megalomaniacal reconstruction of war, staged by a crazy player in a historical re-enactment.

Inside the vehicles, everything is in the miserable Soviet style: cheap plastic, plywood, benches, analogue walkie-talkies, and tinned food that's already out of date. The troops have problems with logistics, provisions, communications – even finding their way. Their maps are all old, from the last century;

the columns find their way by using the street signs, they run out of fuel, get stuck in the mud, and the soldiers go hungry and start looting. Instead of the spruced-up, modernized contract army that Russian propaganda has been repeatedly going on about for years – instead of the army brand with the star that's been spread across Russia by a network of fashionable boutiques selling military merchandise, accompanied by rock festivals and clips commissioned from popular rappers – the world has been shown a disorganized horde without a specific mission, morale or motivation, who do not even know why they have invaded, having been thrown from 'an exercise' into a war of conquest.

The hopeless archaism that has ruled Russian people's minds for the past two decades crawled out into the light like growling tyrannosauruses in the bloody 'Park of the Russian Era'. These dinosaurs snarl with fire, crushing beneath them any cars that get in their way, shooting up any civilian vehicles or inhabitants they happen to see along the road. Russian armoured vehicles are knocked out on the march in whole columns. Drone videos show hundreds of burnt-out vehicles, as if it is the whole aged, metal, mechanical civilization that has been forged in Russia over the past 300 years, from Peter the Great to Vladimir Putin, that has been turned into a pile of scrap metal on the side of Ukrainian roads.

The way in which this war is being fought is also old-fashioned. The bombing of residential areas and the blockading of Ukrainian towns – these are war crimes twentieth-century-style: murder on an industrial scale. The tragedy of Mariupol reminds us of pictures that we have not seen for eighty years: Guernica, Coventry, Stalingrad, Dresden. Yes, since then we have had the extermination by Russian forces of Grozny in Chechnya, and Aleppo in Syria ('we can train there for quite a long time', Putin grinned cynically),[1] but in those places there was not a major attack by ground forces, modelled after the Second World War. Probably when they dreamt up this operation in the Kremlin, they imagined something akin to the war the USA waged in the Persian Gulf in 1991: a high-technology blitzkrieg from the air as a triumph of higher civilization. But it turned out to be clumsy, brutal and ineffective, Russian-style: the Russian army doesn't look like the Americans, but more like the poorly trained and ill-motivated army of Saddam Hussein in 1991, or like the Arab forces in the Six-Day War of 1967, who dumped their Soviet military vehicles and equipment by the thousand in the Sinai Desert.

Finally, the very basis for this war is anachronistic. The trauma of the collapse of the USSR; the post-imperial resentment; the jealousy of a husband thrown over; the delirium about 'one people' of Russians and Ukrainians – these are all the convulsions of the dying Empire, which for more than a hundred years, since 1917, has been unable to pass away. Modern Russia did not just fail to become a nation, it remained a phantom, a ghost of the Russian Empire, a shuffling zombie that has risen from the grave and is terrifying the living. A full-scale war based on a made-up excuse to seize the territory of a neighbour is just monstrous, yet at the same time ridiculous in the twenty-first century, as if those behind it had been reading too many historical novels and pulp fiction about heroes who had come into the present day from the past. Putin's obsession with history has played a cruel trick on him and turned him into an unfortunate character from the past, looking around in amazement at the world of the future.

The war is far from over. The hardest battles still lie ahead; but Russia has already lost. And it is not just the failure of the military operation, but a defeat of Russia's civilization in its collision with Modernity. Russia has cultivated its own archaism for so long, nurturing the notorious 'bonds' and traditional values, performing historical re-enactments and 'Tank Biathlons' (the TV show in which tanks take the place of athletes), dressing up children in soldiers' tunics and creating a cult around the Kalashnikov rifle, that it has produced an antediluvian war, cruel, absurd and ineffective, where tank battalions spend weeks and lose thousands of soldiers fighting over individual houses and farmsteads. Russia has become not just a global threat, but a global laughing-stock. The columns of zombies are still moving along Ukraine's roads and taking with them many human lives, but their time is already running out. When dawn breaks, they will return from whence they came, back to the world of ghosts, shadows and the depths of history.

Revenge of the Underground Man

The alarm bells are ringing in Russia: the country has fallen victim to 'cancel culture'! It appears as if in the West they want to ban all Russian culture in one fell swoop: Chekhov's plays, Tchaikovsky's music and Tolstoy's novels. The patriotic crowd was appalled at one particular case in Milan, where the University of Milano-Bicocca scrapped the Italian writer Paolo Nori's course on Dostoevsky. Propaganda posters went up on billboards in Moscow about it.

But if we are considering Russian culture in the context of the war in Ukraine, it is just as important to look at the other side of the coin: to what extent is it responsible for all of the torture, genocide and terror that is currently being carried out in Ukraine in the name of 'the Russian world'? This is not an idle question, because the Russian leadership justifies the ongoing war against the 'brotherly people' of Ukraine by citing historical and cultural reasons.

Half a century ago, the Czech writer Milan Kundera posed a very similar question. After the Soviet invasion of Czechoslovakia in 1968, he lost his job, and a theatre director whom he knew suggested to him that he write a stage version of Fyodor Dostoevsky's *The Idiot*. Kundera re-read the novel but refused to take on the commission: 'even if I were starving, I could not do the job. Dostoevsky's universe of overblown gestures, murky depths and aggressive sentimentality repelled me', he wrote many years later, in his essay 'An Introduction to a Variation'.[1] As an example, the writer quoted a conversation he had with a Soviet officer in the streets of Prague, who explained the invasion by saying that it showed 'that we love you', and that 'we want to save you from yourselves'. Kundera acknowledged that he was tired of the dark depths of the Russian soul and longed for simple, clear, European rationalism, as in the novels of Denis Diderot.

Six weeks later, none other than the Russian poet Joseph Brodsky replied with indignation to Kundera's diatribe, in the same *New York Times Book Review*. He rejected any responsibility for Soviet (in fact, Russian) imperialism, saying that 'soldiers never represent culture, let alone a literature – they carry guns, not books'.[2]

History repeats itself, and today the same rational logic fails to explain the Russian invasion of Ukraine, refuting all considerations of common sense, strategic calculation and economic interest. This is why many people right up to the last moment, right up until those first missile strikes on the morning of 24 February 2022, did not believe that there could be a war. And just as in 1968, the propagandists continued to talk about 'saving' an occupied country from 'Nazism': one of them, a certain Sergei Markov, even called the Russian missiles destroying Ukrainian cities 'the missiles of Good'.

To understand the roots of this war, once again we need to turn to Dostoevsky, only this time not to *The Idiot* but to *Notes from the Underground*, written in 1864 before the 'Great Pentateuch' of his principal novels. In this programmatic novella, which Nabokov called 'the quintessence of Dostoevskyism', and which influenced the whole of European philosophy, from Friedrich Nietzsche and Max Scheler to Jean-Paul Sartre and Albert Camus, the writer introduced a new character of the late modern era: a resentful neurotic, offended by the world and dreaming of revenge. The protagonist of the story is a short and nondescript clerk who is retired and lives alone in St Petersburg, and who cherishes in his soul his childhood traumas (rejection, lack of friends) and his injury as an adult (an insult from a tall officer in a tavern, who pushed him aside with his shoulder without noticing), and he creates his own underground philosophy based on an irrational concept of free will ('desire').

In an existential impulse, he rejects any projects of human well-being and a rational world order, which is enshrined for him in the Crystal Palace, an enormous exhibition pavilion built in London's Hyde Park for the International Exhibition of 1851, which captured the imagination of his contemporaries. He dreams about destroying it:

> I, for instance, would not be in the least surprised if all of a sudden, *à propos* of nothing, in the midst of general prosperity a gentleman with an ignoble, or rather with a reactionary and ironical, countenance were to arise and, putting his arms akimbo, say to us all: 'I say, gentlemen, hadn't we better kick over the whole show and scatter rationalism to the winds, simply to send these logarithms to the devil, and to enable us to live once more at our own sweet foolish will!'[3]

As the novella progresses, the protagonist suffers more insults, this time from his former classmates, and he takes out his grievances on the meek prostitute Liza, ridiculing and denigrating her.

'The underground man' became one of Dostoevsky's key images. We find his characteristics in Raskolnikov and Svidrigailov in *Crime and Punishment*; in the man-servant Smerdyakov in *The Brothers Karamazov*; and in the terrorist Pyotr Verkhovensky in *The Devils*. The German philosopher Max Scheler, citing Dostoevsky, wrote about 'Russian literature being contaminated with resentment',[4] something echoed by the Russian writer Vasily Rozanov, who wrote that 'the underground man' was a key Russian figure.

Today's Russia has its own 'underground man', a deeply wounded character, an aggrieved neurotic, who nurtures his resentment against the world around him. It is no coincidence that he is a native of St Petersburg, a child of windswept yards and marshy soils: remember with what rapture Dostoevsky's character tells Liza how recently dug graves at the Volkovskoe Cemetery fill up with water. . . . This is the Russian president, Vladimir Putin, who is living underground for the third year in a row: the first two years because of the Covid pandemic, from which he lay low in his bunker and protected himself by placing the strictest possible quarantine on anyone who approached him; and now during the war, according to rumours, he most often hides himself away in a nuclear bomb shelter somewhere beyond the Ural Mountains.

Putin's war in Ukraine is the fruit of an inflamed imagination and a long-standing sense of offence. But Ukraine here is just an excuse, Putin's offence goes much wider: he blames the whole of the West for apparently ignoring Russia ('no one listened to us before . . . just listen to us now', he said at the unveiling of a new type of nuclear weapon in 2018); for their arrogance and the sense of a civilizational superiority. This is the same hatred as that of 'the underground man' for the Crystal Palace, the cynical nihilism of a man who does not believe in altruism and the common good.

'The Bunker Man' has thrown out a challenge to the whole modern world order. For well over a decade, this has become a fixed idea in the heads of Putin's ideologists, from the freak economists such as Sergei Glazyev and Mikhail Delyagin, to the outwardly decent Valdai Club and the Council for Foreign and Defence Policy.[5] They all claimed that the world order led by the USA and the West had become weak and rotten, that Russia should take upon itself the role of finishing it off and on its ruins establish a 'multi-polar world', in which Russia itself would hold a prestigious place. This is the suicidal act of 'the underground man', who wishes to destroy the Crystal Palace and 'to live once more at our own sweet foolish will', who wants to turn his inferiority complex into a Herostratus complex, fanning the flames of a global fire.

The war in Ukraine is seen as one stage in the elimination of norms, rules and institutions. It was meant to show the insignificance of NATO, the European Union, the Organization for Security and Cooperation in Europe (OSCE), the United Nations and the trans-Atlantic partnership in the face of a Russian attack, and the inability of the West to display a united front. And even the failure of the blitzkrieg and the unprecedented level of sanctions have not weakened the Kremlin's grim determination to smash the old world; if anything, they have just strengthened it. The Russian leadership is now in a state of euphoria about this 'historic moment', the global collapse of rules and norms, fascinated by the pernicious Karamazov-esque idea that 'everything is permitted'. Having ruined not only a neighbouring state but his own country's future, too, 'the underground man' with the nuclear button is now threatening to destroy the whole world.

. . . After the row it caused, the course on Dostoevsky that was banned at Milan University was returned the next day to the course list. No one in the West is going to ban Russian culture, which is now methodically banning itself.

The Z Virus

Like a bat carrying Covid, it has sneaked into our life, our dreams, our fears, spreading like a virus with its sharp spikes, tearing the fabric of our existence, leaving its deadly marks everywhere. The letter 'Z' instantly became the symbol of Russia's war against Ukraine – oh, let's not be modest: against the whole world. It seizes the visual space of our cities, the facades of buildings, shop windows, the sides of buses and car bumpers, but, most of all, the rear doors of battered 'Gazelles', urban delivery trucks, where someone has written this letter with their finger in the dirt. Prisoners in their exercise yards and youngsters in children's homes are lined up in Z-formation for drone photographs; books are laid out in a Z-shape on the shelves of libraries; and the windows of administrative buildings are lit up at night in the form of the letter 'Z'.[1] In Kemerovo in the Kuzbass Region, the governor, Sergei Tsivilyov, ordered that in all official documents the region's name should be written 'KuZbass'. Russia has been gripped by the Z fever.

What does this symbol mean? Military specialists say that from the start of the war these were the signs chosen to mark vehicles of the western and eastern groups of forces for the invasion of Ukraine: 'Z' for *zapad* ['west'], and 'V' for *vostok* ['east']. But, whatever these letters are supposed to signify, the instant promotion of 'Z', the appearance of thousands of billboards and quality pictures taken by drones of Z-performances, the fervour with which officials put it on the facades of public buildings, all point to a massive PR campaign, thought out well before the start of the war and, it seems, approved by the Kremlin. But still, why the Latin letter 'Z'? Why were the sharp foreign letters Z and V chosen as the symbols of 'the Russian world', for the return of Ukraine to the bosom of Slav unity, for a battle with the Western disease of 'Nazism'?

After all, for nearly twenty years Russia has had its own homegrown symbol, the St George's ribbon, which, as a sign of identity, often replaced the Russian flag. From the point of view of image, this was a successful visual symbol: the ribbon joined the heroes of the past ('our grandfathers fought', as a propaganda meme runs) with the revanchist present ('Russia, rising from its knees').[2] It united the generations and the different classes in society that had been torn apart by mistrust and social inequality; it was a bandage to heal hurt national pride. It fulfilled the same function as the red cord on the fasces, the Roman lictor tuft (a rod with an axe, tied with a ribbon), that was chosen as the symbol of Italian fascism and gave it its name. In the primary sense, fascism is the bonding of society, the policy of binding, the principle of all-encompassing togetherness known in Russian as *sobornost* ['conciliarity']; this is a favourite Russian word of Orthodox thinkers and Russian patriots, but could also serve as a suitable translation for the term 'fascism'.

It was exactly this sort of Mediterranean fascism, with its paternalistic state, its obedient oligarchs, its cult of the past and the propaganda of war, that had been building in Russia for the last few decades – just the sort of corporate fascism that made people line up in administrative formations (a sector for each government department) at official rallies in support of the annexation of Crimea in 2014, or march in columns with generic portraits of Second World War heroes in processions of the 'Immortal Regiment'. It is the sort of fascism that killed the journalist Anastasia Baburova and the lawyer Stanislav Markelov, the journalist Anna Politkovskaya and the politician Boris Nemtsov (some of the well-known victims of political murders during Putin's time in office); and then sent its stormtroopers to break up the people's memorial to Nemtsov on the Moskvoretsky Bridge in Moscow, the site of his murder; the sort of fascism that made kitschy patriotic films and banned theatrical performances and exhibitions of what it considered 'degenerate art'. Society was wrapped together with the ribbon of St George, like goods in a celebratory display in the window of a shop on the eve of Victory Day.

But the sharp 'Z' sign cut through this ribbon on 24 February 2022. It brought not peace but a sword, and heralded a resolute break with the past. Indeed, this is the main idea behind the war in Ukraine: it is a radical gesture of rejection, of Russia's removing itself from the tide of history and the logic of international relations; it is an act demonstrating the destruction of conventions. This is what the Kremlin was trying to do for a long time – to change the rules and radically reshape the world order, which it considered was unfair to Russia. This was why an unprecedented military operation on land was launched, something of a size not seen since the Second World War, and for its symbol they took a sign that signalled a break with tradition, even with the actual Russian alphabet. It is no coincidence that Z is the last letter of the Latin alphabet, followed by emptiness, zero, the end.

Observers noted its similarity with Nazi symbolism: Z reminds one that the *Wolfsangel* runic sign was the tactical badge of the Fourth SS Division that fought at Luga, Pskov and Leningrad, and the 133rd Festungs Division of the Wehrmacht. It is difficult to imagine that this is exactly what the Russian spin doctors had in mind when they were working out a visual image for their 'denazification' operation, but by a diabolical irony the

Russian symbol of war was unfailingly recognized as being a Nazi symbol. The semiotics of the Z sign illustrate the switch from the fascism of the 'traditional bonds' of the past decade to a chemically clean Nazism. It is the idea of the superiority of the Russian race over the ethnicity of the Ukrainians, which, according to Putin's pseudo-historical essays, and manifestoes like the odious pamphlet written by Timofei Sergeytsev,[3] does not have its own subjectivity, or a right to nationhood, statehood, culture, language or independent existence. In the new Russian ideology, Ukrainians have taken the place that the Jews were given by the Nazis, and it seems that the aim of this war is the *Endlösung*, 'the final solution', of the Ukrainian question, which has become the Russian president's obsession.

But, unexpectedly, the semi-swastika captured the imagination of Russians and spread throughout the country, leaving its mark everywhere, rather like Zorro, who drew the letter with his rapier on the skin of his victims. It went from being a propaganda meme to a national emblem: the ideology of destruction, denial and nullification. The letter 'Z' has been stuck on Russia's principal symbols – church cupolas, Easter cakes (the Patriarch had to come out with a special explanation, asking believers not to do this), on the red star and on that ribbon of St George. The parade on May 9, 2022 also took place under the Z sign, which rather meant that it lost its meaning: the victors over Nazism in 1945 carrying out a parade under the 2022 Nazi symbol. They use the Z sign to mark out the enemies of 'the Reich' by drawing it on their doors. This happened to the film critic Anton Dolin, the theatre critic Marina Davydova, the Pussy Riot member Rita Flores, and other public figures who dared to disagree with the war. Thugs sprayed the Z on the walls of the headquarters of the Moscow branch of the Memorial organization, which stood up for human rights and defending the memory of Russia's history. The organization was closed down and liquidated in the first weeks of the war.

In fact, the thick Z sign has been drawn in paint and blood all over Russia, wiping out all the life that has grown up in this space over the last thirty years: the market economy, civil society, a web of connections with the outside world and hopes for the future. With a loud crash, Russia is breaking away from its own past, from everyday life, from global civilization; and there is something infernal in this picture of voluntary eager self-destruction. This can best be described by one of Dostoevsky's favourite phrases: 'stripped naked'. Russia has stripped itself naked in this sadomasochistic ecstasy of war; it has no pants on, just a T-shirt on which is written, 'I'm not ashamed.'[4]

On the point of sadomasochism: apparently the spin doctors who came up with the Z symbol had a peculiar sense of humour, and remembered well Quentin Tarantino's film *Pulp Fiction*, and the perverted Zed in leather and latex on a Harley with a Z-shaped keychain. One of the best scenes in the film (actually, are there any bad ones?) is the final dialogue between Butch Coolidge (played by Bruce Willis) and his girlfriend, Fabienne:

> Fabienne: Whose motorcycle is this?
> Butch: It's a chopper, baby.
> Fabienne: Whose chopper is this?
> Butch: It's Zed's.
> Fabienne: Who's Zed?
> Butch: Zed's dead, baby. Zed's dead.

I cannot think of any better answer to the question: What does the Z symbol mean?

Russia Inside Out

An Anthropological Catastrophe

As the war proceeds, it becomes more difficult to be surprised or horrified by what we are learning of it. But then fresh evidence emerges of the brutality of the Russian army and once again you tumble into the abyss. At the start of April 2022 in the village of Termakhivka in the Kyiv Oblast, Russian soldiers seized five local lads, tied them up, laid them in a circle on the ground, and kept them like that for fifteen days with a machine-gun pointing at them. At night, the temperature fell to minus 10 Celsius and snow fell – which the lads ate from the ground. One of them raised himself up a little and as a result was shot in the leg. He lay there with an open wound and his leg began to rot. At one time the soldiers dragged up 'a 200',[1] the corpse of a local resident they had killed, and threw it into the middle of the circle, saying, 'That's so you can sleep well.'

It is unlikely that these soldiers would have watched the film *Cargo-200*, by the cult director Alexei Balabanov, who predicted among other things the rise of Russian fascism; but no doubt the late director would have envied their perverted fantasy.[2] In Ukraine, an orgy of epic, boundless violence continues to take place, with mass shootings and savage acts of torture. Residents have been killed just for the fun of it, out of boredom or for entertainment; parents have been raped and murdered in front of their children, and the other way round; there has been violence against girls and women aged from 8 to 80. It is excruciating to read such evidence, yet it is essential from a duty to feel compassion and empathy – but also, to try to understand such tortures. Where does such terrible evil come from as that which has been brought by the Russian army – from what chthonic depths, from which nightmares and horror films? Has a genetic mutation, an anthropological catastrophe, occurred in Russia, which produced such indifferent sadists, who have now marched onto Ukrainian territory? Those residents who survived and witnessed their brutality now talk about them less with fear than with amazement: 'We have never seen this before'; 'We could never even have imagined that such things were possible.'

Indeed, one does not have to be Fyodor Dostoevsky, Yury Mamleyev or Vladimir Sorokin[3] to delve into the darker recesses of the Russian soul. All you need to do is look at a list of police brutality, tortures that take place in police stations and corrective colonies, or the crimes committed by the army, to understand that what has gone on in Bucha, Irpen and other towns and villages that have fallen under Russian occupation is not excessive or pathological but part of the norm, the everyday behaviour of the Russian apparatus of violence. Journalists from the Russian investigative publication *Proyekt* dug up the history of the Russian units that were stationed in Bucha (the name of this small town near Kyiv has become well known because of the brutal acts committed there), and they found that the units sent there are infamous for their cruelty in peacetime, too. For example, the 64th Motorized Rifle Brigade of the 35th Army from Khabarovsk in the Far East of Russia enjoys a sinister reputation even in its home region, so that parents scare the kids with its call-sign, 'Mlechnik'. Suicides are regular occurrences there; conscripts and contract soldiers desert from there; in a period of just three weeks in March 2014, seven people died in military unit 51460, based in the village of Knyazye-Volkonskoye. It is worth noting that, after the Russian army withdrew from the area near Kyiv, President Putin granted this unit the honorary title of 'Guards', as if rewarding them for the war crimes that they had committed. The same reputation for violence accompanies the 127th Motorized Rifle Division of the 5th Army, also based in the Far East: they regularly appear in criminal proceedings, and the headless corpses of soldiers have been found in the area where the unit is based. These were not some special monsters who were operating in Bucha (there were rumours about Chechen sub-units, which were also noted for their cruel acts), but ordinary Russian army units that use violence as their standard operating procedure.

From Grozny to Mariupol

Russia's war crimes in Ukraine are in no way unique. In my generation's living memory, there has been the slaughter of Bosnian Muslims in Srebrenica, and Saddam Hussein's use of chemical weapons against the Kurds in Iraq. There was the genocide of a million Tutsis in Rwanda, and the continuing extermination of the Uighurs in the Chinese province of Xinjiang. What is more, when we look at our own recent history, the same methods were used in Chechnya in 1994–6 and 1999–2004 (likewise, these were not called 'wars' but 'operations to restore constitutional order'), and in Syria in 2015: the bombing of civilian targets (the destruction of residential areas in the Syrian city of Aleppo), and *zachistki*, the 'cleansing' of the villages, remind us of the Chechen villages of Novye Aldy or Samashki, in each of which up to 100 civilians were killed. These crimes passed by, being of little concern to our public consciousness, except for a tiny group of human rights advocates. They did not become subjects for wide discussion or judicial review or stay in our memory – in the same way that the 1 million Afghans who lost their lives during the Soviet occupation of Afghanistan from 1979 to 1989 were forgotten.

Jeff Hawn from the London School of Economics (LSE), who has studied the question of violence in the Russian army, notes that the war crimes committed by that army in the twenty-first century have gone unpunished – from Chechnya and Georgia to Syria and the Donbas since 2014. Unlike Western armies, the Russian armed forces have not developed an institutional-ized culture that would enable them to minimize losses among the civilian population; the Russian army has no safeguards against unjustified and arbitrary violence. 'The brutality we see in today's Russian army is born out of its organic inability to rid itself of the legacy of its Soviet predecessor', he concludes; 'Lethality and victory at any price remain the main priorities for the Russian military.'[4]

Indeed, Russian generals have traditionally regarded army personnel as cannon fodder. Just as in Chechnya many years ago, the army has been thrown into this bloody mincing machine, with its columns shot up on the move, and its tanks and armoured personnel carriers sent into the middle of built-up areas, where they are sitting targets and their crews are burnt alive in their metal boxes. What has Chernobayevka alone cost, a small town near Kherson with a population of 8,000 inhabitants, where there was an aerodrome of strate-gic importance for the Russian forces? The Russian army has seized it and then retreated at least 14 times, losing in the process up to 50 helicopters, 100 tanks and hundreds of sol-diers and officers, including 2 lieutenant-generals, according to Ukrainian accounts. Chernobayevka has become a meme, synonymous with Russian military failures, the incompetence of the military commanders and their indifference to losses of personnel. The same happened in late 2022, when the Russian troops – most notably the regiments of the Wagner private military company, staffed by recruited Russian prisoners – for weeks stormed the small towns of Bakhmut and Soledar in Donetsk Oblast, losing, by Ukrainian accounts, thousands of soldiers.

This is reminiscent of scenes from the Great Patriotic War: from the Nevsky Spot near Leningrad, where a quarter of a million Soviet soldiers lost their lives on a tiny bridgehead in 1941–3, to the reckless frontal storming by Marshal Zhukov of the Seelow Heights close to Berlin in 1945, where over the course of four days 40,000 soldiers laid down their lives in this small town. The German machine-gunners are known to have lost their minds, unable to deal with killing scores of Soviet soldiers day after day. Today, this pattern is being repeated in Russia's suicidal war in Ukraine.

The Russian Overcoat

Violence in Russia is not limited to the institutions of the state. It happens in families, in relations between men and women, between the old and the young. It has been heard in intercepted telephone conversations between Russian soldiers and their commanders, which abound with swearing, threats and insults; in phone calls and correspondence between soldiers and their families, where tearful sentimentality is mixed with cruelty and cynicism: mothers advise their soldier sons what of value is worth taking from Ukrainian homes, and what size footwear to bring back from there; a wife tells her officer husband, 'Go ahead and rape the Ukrainian bitches, just take precautions.' Violence has become part of the flesh and blood of Russian society; it has become its source code, built on hierarchy and subordination, on the grabbing and distribution of resources, where brute strength is more important than morality, and the authorities are above the law. This order is consecrated by the behaviour of the ruling class, using their cars with blue lights to brush aside the ordinary people, going unpunished by the legal system, and being blessed by President Putin's speeches, which teach that 'The weak get beaten' and 'You have to strike first', greeted by wild applause from the crowd.

As a rule, this violence has been reserved for internal use, to support and legitimize the social and political order in the country; but now it has spread beyond Russia's borders on a massive scale, with an invading army, sanctioned by the state and given an ideological basis. The occupying soldiers have taken literally Putin's words about Ukraine being run by 'Nazis and drug-addicts', which he picked up from propaganda (it seems that this is his basic source of information on the world outside his bunker), and these soldiers burst into Ukrainian homes and ask the shocked residents: 'Where are the Nazis, then?!' Or, as the inhabitants of the aforementioned Termakhivka, near Kyiv, can testify, the surprised soldiers say, 'We cut off all the old man's fingers and he didn't say a word – he has to be a drug addict!' In attempting to understand what is behind the brutality of the Russian occupiers of Ukraine, we can see that the problem lies not with individual sadists or hooligans, but in the very structure of the Russian state and society.

To put it simply, Russia is sewn like an overcoat. Not like Bashmachkin's[5] overcoat from Nikolai Gogol's story, one of the key texts of Russian literature, but the basic soldier's overcoat, one of the fundamental archetypes of a nation that is constantly at war. It has an outside and an inner lining. The outside is harsh, rough, and has been scuffed over the centuries: the endless space, the sheer size, the Empire, wars, tanks and aircraft, the atomic bomb, Sputnik and the Space programme, Tolstoy and Dostoevsky, the imperial splendour of Moscow and St Petersburg, cathedrals and palaces. On the inside, which the world does not see, but that we wear against our bodies, there is slavery, boorishness, theft, lies, tyranny and the inescapable cruelty of Russian life. We have grown used to this, squirming and scratching; certain patriots even consider that that is the price of greatness, and are even proud that this is how Russian life is: the roof may leak and there may be no toilet or running water in the house, but for all that there is classical ballet, nineteenth-century literature, the mysterious Russian soul and the Great Empire.

But now things have become muddled; the overcoat has been turned inside out, and this base squalor has been revealed for all to see in the shape of the 'invading army'. All of Russia's senseless malice, dense ignorance, wholesale theft, cruelty, violence and disdain for personal dignity and human life have been revealed to the world. All those typical national features that we considered our own and that we have grown used to inside the country suddenly became visible. All the holes, tears, crooked seams and half-rotten fabric of the Russian over-coat have been exposed. This is a catastrophe not of Russia's reputation, but of its very civilization. It ruins the power of simulation on which Russia has been premised for the past few centuries: Russia has been exposed to the world exactly as it is. We Russians may be horrified by that abysmal evil that has been displayed in Bucha and Mariupol, but we should not be surprised: all of Russia is our Bucha.[6]

Mobilization as Russian Fate

History Re-visited

'We Can Repeat It!' Russian propaganda has been churning out for a good twenty years. Finally, it has happened: Russian history has repeated itself in all its glory and disgrace. The first 'partial' mobilization took place in Russia in late 2022, and its pictures are painstakingly familiar from the classics of Russian literature and war films. Crowds of men of various ages, young and middle-aged (although you even see some grey-haired ones), dressed in civilian clothes, carrying rucksacks and awkward trunks, some looking brave, others distressed, accompanied by their nearest and dearest, huddle together before the doors of the recruiting office, or are already on the platform awaiting the train's departure. Children are crying, the women silently wipe away tears, those called up smoke and pass round the vodka bottle (many of them are already very drunk); the orchestra clumsily strikes up 'Farewell of Slavianka', the Russian military march from 1912, symbolizing troops going off to war; and a podgy, bearded priest blesses the war and waves his cross over them.

Without looking back, one after another they disappear into the black hole of the recruiting office or the railway carriage.

Within a couple of weeks, or maybe even days, wearing some sort of uniform and armed with a rusty Kalashnikov rifle from the strategic reserve stock, and without going through any training and with no coordination, they will be thrown over the borderline, the so-called 'ribbon', into Ukraine. They will be dumped into trenches or stuck in revamped armoured vehicles that are half a century old and start up occasionally, and sent to kill Ukrainians or themselves be killed: to be burnt up in these metal boxes, to lie in the black earth of Ukraine, or to rot in the hospitals of Rostov, having lost their legs. The economists Oleg Itskhoki and Maxim Mironov have calculated that the expected losses among these new raw recruits will be much higher than for the regular army; they will be comparable to the losses in the forces of the so-called 'Donetsk People's Republic', where, according to British intelligence, such losses make up 55 per cent of the troop numbers. Itskhoki and Mironov reckon that, in the next six months, losses among the mobilized Russian troops will amount to 60 to 70 per cent, with 15–20 per cent killed and 45–50 per cent wounded. Spin, Russian roulette!

The authorities grab people indiscriminately. In the city of Ulan-Ude, in the Baikal Region, students were taken from their lectures. In Bashkiria, the entire philharmonic orchestra was called up. In the town of Zelenograd, near Moscow, hundreds of workers from the microelectronics plant were called up, including those employed by 'Angstrem' and 'Mikron', companies that make microchips for the military, leading the directors to write letters in panic to the Defence Ministry, complaining that they were destroying a strategic sector. Call-up notices have been sent to judges and prosecutors, those who have served in the army and those who have not, lads of 18 years of age and – against all the rules – men of 60, as happened on a mass scale in Buryatia. And in the village of Tyumenevo in the Kemerovo Oblast in Siberia, the entire male population – fifty-nine men – was called up.

This brings to mind images of the mobilization for the Russo-Japanese War in the spring of 1904, as described by Leo Tolstoy in his well-known article 'Bethink Yourselves!' (*Opomnites'!*):

> Stupefied by prayers, sermons, exhortations, by processions, pictures, and newspapers, the cannon's flesh, hundreds of thousands of men, uniformly dressed, carrying divers deadly weapons, leaving their parents, wives, 7 children, with hearts of agony, but with artificial sprightliness, go where they, risking their own lives, will commit the most dreadful act of killing men whom they do not know and who have done them no harm.[1]

The worst aspect of Russian history repeats itself, century after century, churning out scenes of state cruelty, bureaucratic lawlessness and human submissiveness.

Mining for People

The character of the call-up (which is as much 'partial' as the war in Ukraine is a 'special operation') reveals all the innate traits of the Russian socio-political structure that have matured under Putin and been institutionalized. The first of these is to regard the people as raw material: treating the population as a renewable natural resource is firmly embedded in the mind of Putin's elite. For some years now, the state has pushed forward its demographic priorities, battling against LGBT and the child-free movement, banning abortion and pushing 'family values'. At the same time, the state increased the pressure on the population to try to get as much as possible out of people. The Russian people saw the removal of the social services provided in Soviet times; budget cuts and the commercialization of education and healthcare; the raising of the pension age;

and the imposition of greater taxation on business, which was then passed on to the shoulders of the consumers. The unprecedented stratification of society pushed millions of people and whole regions below the poverty line, just as the authorities were promoting the idea that the population should live modestly and economically – in effect, using poverty as an instrument of political control over large masses of people.

And now the biopolitics of power turns into the thanatopolitics of mobilization. Firstly, the poorest regions and the lowest social strata were offered contracts to sign up for the army (this was used in particular in relation to the most hapless category of the population, prisoners, whom the so-called 'Putin's chef', Yevgeny Prigozhin, recruits into the Wagner private military company to use as cannon fodder).[2] Now, millions more find themselves under threat of being enlisted, to use their bodies to fill the gaps in the frontline, to act as expendable material in a failed war. In doing this, the state is observing the social and territorial hierarchy of Russian society. There has been mass mobilization of the population on the edges of the country: the Far East, the Baikal Region and long-suffering Buryatia in East Siberia, which was subject to an almost complete, 'carpet mobilization', leading local human rights activists to talk of 'the genocide of the Buryat people'. (The same thing has happened with the Crimean Tatars, the repressed national minority in Crimea, annexed by Russia in 2014, where 90 per cent of men have been called up – a clearly political order.) Yet the areas considered critical for the authorities, Moscow and St Petersburg, have seen far less mobilization – the plan for Moscow, with its population of 15 million, was to draft just 16,000 people: 0.1 per cent. In the same way, the propagandists in state media or those working in the banks that are important for the system are excused the draft. People's value is determined by how close they are to the centre of power.

Meanwhile, the use of the human body is distinguished by typical Russian inefficiency and wastefulness. They call up more people than are needed; they are sent off randomly, housed in unsuitable accommodation without food or amenities; ordered to buy their own camouflage equipment, body armour and helmets. A video spread on the Internet in which a female officer advised draftees to buy women's panty-liners to put into their leaking boots, and tampons to use as compresses for bullet wounds. All of this is part of the ideology of 'inexhaustible human resources', summed up in the aphorism, 'the women will bear more of them', allegedly said by Marshal Zhukov.[3] But in this excess lies the essence of the state machinery of terror, by which it demonstrates its omnipotence. Mobilization has much in common with state terror as an instrument of repression used to discipline the human biomass.

The state acts on the logic of big numbers. So, what if 100,000 or 200,000 Russian soldiers die in Ukraine (as apparently has been budgeted for by the Russian Ministry of Finance to make funeral payments to the families of military personnel killed in 2022 and 2023, according to a leak published by Mikhail Khodorkovsky)? Or maybe it could be a million, like the number of surplus deaths in Russia during the Covid pandemic? But what is that compared to the prize of 8 million extra people taken into Russia from Crimea and the occupied regions of Eastern Ukraine? A resource approach to the population has its own arithmetic.

Resigned to Fate

The second thing that has traditionally been part of the Russian contract between power and society was also displayed when the mobilization was ordered: the overwhelming obedience of the population and their readiness to go and kill and be killed for unclear reasons at the behest of the state. True, there are tens of thousands of people who do not agree and are fearless, and who went on the streets to protest against the war when the mobilization was announced. Thousands of them were held and charged (some also being given their call-up papers at the police station). There are hundreds of thousands who made a dash for the borders of neighbouring countries: Finland and Georgia, Mongolia and Kazakhstan, some even taking boats from Chukotka to Alaska across the Bering Straits . . . and tens of thousands more who left for Armenia, Azerbaijan, Uzbekistan, Turkey, Israel and a number of other countries. The exodus from Russia in the first two weeks after the call-up was announced is estimated at 800,000 people. Even so, the number of people who openly protested on the streets or voted with their feet at the borders was less than 1 per cent of the population; so the rest – and we are talking here about millions of people – accepted the call-up as a part of normal life and the rules of the game, and went off to the recruitment offices or tried to find some way of obtaining an exemption. Generally speaking, if we take Albert Hirschman's triad of 'Exit–Voice–Loyalty', we can say that a fraction of a per cent opted to raise their 'Voice'; half a per cent chose 'Exit'; and the rest, voluntarily or involuntarily, went for 'Loyalty'.[4]

Make no mistake, it is a statistically insignificant minority who have gone to Ukraine with a clear motivation 'to fight the Nazis', but the majority are simply not prepared to stand up to the will of the state (despite the fact that refusing, or simply avoiding, to accept the call-up papers is liable to a tiny punishment – a fine of 500 to 3,000 roubles, which is 10–50 US dollars). The Internet is full of stories of people who went to the recruitment office as soon as they were contacted; of parents who sent their children off to war, 'so that we didn't have problems with the cops'; of bosses who report their workforce to recruiters; and of people who were excused service but still went off to fight, because 'They'd drafted my brothers', or 'We'd be embarrassed in front of the neighbours', or simply because 'I felt awkward in front of my mates.' It is as if for the Russian the fear of the state (be it the boss in state service, the military recruiting office, the police or the head of a higher educational establishment) is greater than the fear of death. This is to say nothing of the idea that, at the authorities' order, people are prepared not only to die, but to kill – the moral component is not considered at all. Just as in the spring and summer of 2022 there was a process of normalization of the war in Russia, in the autumn of 2022 there has been a normalization of the call-up. The war is now taking place not only on TV screens, but in everyone's homes, and except for that 1 per cent that has protested or emigrated, the population bows down and submits to the will of the state.

And it is not just about 'the average man', but about the elite, too – managers, big business, oligarchs and the higher bureaucrats. All of them unquestioningly fell into line, first behind the idea of the 'special military operation', then behind the idea of a general war and mobilization. All these people, who went through the ordeal of the 'stormy nineties', with its criminal and business wars, who fought for their property, made a position and a state career for themselves – all of them, including the 'liberals within the system' and the global entrepreneurs, have humbly laid their achievements, their resources and their reputations on the altar of the war and do not demonstrate (publicly, at least) the slightest disagreement. We are talking now not only about the total de-politicization of the Russian population and the elite, but about the total lack of subjectivity. Apart from a few marginal groups of protesters, people have given in to the state and are incapable of opposing it by collective or individual action – the only alternative strategies are evasion or outright escape.

The reason for this is the totality of the Russian state that Putin has re-created in the twenty-first century, with a 70 per cent state-controlled economy, the feudal structure of society, the 'nationalized' elite, and the conformist and divided population. The state in Russia has effectively destroyed society and the fundamentals of citizenship; everyone is trapped in their own cell of the corporate and territorial structure, and owes all the elements of their life not to their own merits, but to the state, which distributes benefits, privileges – and repression. The individual looks at the world through the eyes of the state; and the state logic, *raison d'État*, especially in anything related to questions of security, is placed above the individual identity; and the businessman and the manager submissively jump on the bandwagon of 'mobilization', and with a sense of doom the draftee grabs his duffel bag. The idea of quitting this paradigm, of saying 'no!' to the state (to the boss, to the military recruiter, to the policeman) arises in just a few; and it must be admitted that this submissiveness and lack of subjectivity is a huge achievement of Putin's rule, considering how unruly and anarchic the country was back in the 1990s.

This is also a sign of the effectiveness of the repressive machinery that has been built in Russia over the past decade. And with the way in which demonstrations have been brutally broken up, the acts of torture that take place in police stations and the thousands of unjust sentences that have been passed, people have learnt to fear in a way that had been forgotten since Soviet times. The 'unwhipped generation' who have been born and grown up under Putin absorbed this learned helplessness with the spirit of the time, and along with their parents they suffer from 'Stockholm Syndrome'.[5] As mentioned above, strategies exist for protest, evasion and escape; but these are incapable of stopping the faceless machinery of mobilization and state terror.

The Russian Culture of Death

And the final point: anthropologists and social psychologists have yet to investigate this phenomenon, but Russian society seems to have taken the edge off the fear of death. It is quite possible that the coronavirus pandemic played a part in this, as it showed that a significant part of society is governed by fatalism and indifference ('if you're going to die, you'll die'), coupled with contempt for their own safety and the safety of others ('*I'm* not going to be vaccinated, and I won't give one to my child, either'). The indifference that the population displayed towards the million-plus deaths from Covid convinced the authorities that victims were acceptable and that there is a high tolerance threshold in society. It appears that the population relates to the call-up and the war itself in a similar way to how it regarded the pandemic: as an external force, and a fate that must be obeyed. In each case, people were presented with a choice: to respond to the emergency situation (have a vaccination, refuse the call-up or leave the country), or not to change anything and accept the risk of death (not to get vaccinated, accept the call-up); and people chose to do nothing and to risk dying. In many Internet forums and chats, people calmly write about the deaths of their loved ones – it is as if Putin managed to infect the whole population of Russia with his rhetoric about death ('We'll go to heaven, while they [the West – SM] will just expire'; 'Why do we need the world if there's no Russia in it?' and so on).[6]

Whence this obedience to the state, whence this fatalism in the face of death? We could talk about serfdom and 'internal colonization' of the people by the state, about the eternal collectivism of the Russian peasant community [*obshchina*] and the triumph in Russia of the imperative of survival over self-expression (as per Ronald Inglehart).[7] We could argue whether there is a 'Russian path' and if Russia could get out of it. But the fact remains that the Russian Leviathan has succeeded in resurrecting the traditional patterns of power and the relationship between the state and society. The mobilization cart has set off, creaking and screeching, losing people on the way, kneading the mud with its wheels, and somehow it got going to the sound of a squealing accordion and a woman's tears. Rather like Stalin at the Victory banquet in May 1945, Putin could raise a glass to the great Russian people and their unprecedented patience.[8] But, unlike Stalin, he will not have a victory parade.

The Age of the Sledgehammer

One of the main symbols of Russia in 2022 has been the sledgehammer – the very same instrument as the one that apparently was used to execute the recruited prisoner Yevgeny Nuzhin, who was apprehended after fleeing from the Wagner private military company. In a video entitled 'The Hammer of Vengeance', which was put out on one of the Telegram channels that is close to Wagner, there are excerpts from an interview with the ex-prisoner, in which he tells how he voluntarily surrendered so that he could switch sides and fight with the Ukrainians. Next, Nuzhin himself appears in shot, lying on his side with his head taped down to a rock. Then someone out of shot smashes his face in with a sledgehammer. In the end credits of the film clip, Nuzhin is called a traitor, who 'received the archetypally traditional Wagner punishment'. Wagner's founder, Yevgeny Prigozhin, confirmed that the video was authentic. 'I think this film should be called, "a dog receives a dog's death"', he said; 'It's a beautifully made film.'

The deliberate cruelty shown in this video and the way it was broadcast extensively demonstrate a well-planned PR act intended to have the widest possible coverage. The Wagner soldiers are infamous for their torturing and extrajudicial executions, such as the murder in Syria in 2016 of Hamdi Taha al-Bouti. He had deserted the Syrian government forces, and a video shows him being beaten with a sledgehammer, mutilated, hung and then set on fire, accompanied by the jolly commentary of those who took part in the execution. It seems that this video appeared on social media by chance, because some of the murderers even take off their masks, enabling them to be identified. But the film showing Yevgeny Nuzhin's punishment was deliberately published, rather like the other Prigozhin video three months earlier, in which the so-called 'Putin's chef' himself, in a business-like way, recruits into the Wagner group prisoners in one of Russia's labour camps, while prison staff stand by indifferently.

The video of the punishment contains a strong message, and one that is not just for the former prisoners who are fighting with Wagner and might be thinking about surrendering (it appears that there are ever more such instances). It is aimed also at the entire Russian population, first and foremost the *siloviki* and other representatives of the elite. In a separate statement issued through his press service, Prigozhin talks about 'the traitors in their high offices and their personal business jets'. It was notable that, around the same time, Prigozhin went on the attack against his long-time opponent, another of Putin's protégés and the governor of St Petersburg, Alexander Beglov. Prigozhin wrote to the FSB and the prosecutor general, asking them to investigate Beglov under the constitutional article on 'high treason'.

This demonstrative act with the sledgehammer finally reserves for Prigozhin his private zone of illegitimate violence, like the one already enjoyed for a long time by the head of Chechnya, Ramzan Kadyrov. Kadyrov has exempted his republic from the jurisdiction of the Russian Constitution or Russian law; in Chechnya, he practises Sharia law, extrajudicial executions and hostage-taking, and even prevents representatives from the federal law-enforcement bodies from setting foot on his territory. Prigozhin is constructing his own 'Wagner republic', where lawlessness reigns, mercenaries are actively hired (in contravention of Article 170 of the Russian Criminal Code), illegal military formations are created (in contravention of Article 208), and similar extrajudicial executions are carried out. Now he has wormed his way deep into the prison system and is recruiting prisoners, particularly those with longer prison terms who have been convicted of serious and especially grave offences. He removes them from their places of detention, giving them unsubstantiated promises of release and that their criminal record will be expunged if they spend six months fighting for the Wagner group. By doing so, he is undermining the Russian law-enforcement system, nullifying the work of thousands of operatives, investigators, prosecutors, judges and employees of the Federal Penitentiary Service. According to statistics published by 'Mediazona', the number of prisoners in Russian labour camps in September and October 2022 fell by 23,000, from almost 349,000 to 325,000. There has never been such a drop in numbers since 2010. Even the most widespread amnesties in recent years have not released so many prisoners in such a short period.

At the same time, Prigozhin himself deliberately humiliates the law-enforcement agencies. In a mocking letter sent to the prosecutor general, Igor Krasnov, he maintained that executed defector Yevgeny Nuzhin had indeed fought as a volunteer in Ukraine, but also that he was an American agent who was recruited by the CIA and 'was jailed in advance for 27 years' in order subsequently to infiltrate the Wagner group. He is addressing not only the *siloviki*, but also his patron, Vladimir Putin: Prigozhin is presenting this sledgehammer to the president as evidence of his omnipotence and impunity, in the same way that, seven years ago, similar evidence was presented near the Kremlin walls when the opposition politician Boris Nemtsov was shot[1] – in the higher echelons of Russian power, there are brutal medieval ways of sending important messages. The Presidential Administration helplessly threw up their hands: Putin's press secretary, Dmitry Peskov, said that he didn't know to what extent the video featuring Nuzhin reflected what actually happened, and added 'It's nothing to do with us.' Peskov's words are evidence of the Kremlin's powerlessness before Prigozhin; or, perhaps more accurately, that he has been given carte blanche to do as he wishes.

The actions of 'Putin's chef' are a perfect indication of just how far the contemporary state has unravelled in Russia. It has lost its fundamental monopoly on violence and turned into a *signoria* from the Middle Ages, in which the ruler did not have the unconditional right of the sovereign. And Prigozhin looks like a *condottiere*, a soldier of fortune, the commander of a band of mercenaries in medieval Italy, who would make *Condotta* agreements to carry out military operations, paying his fighters in *soldi* money (from where we have the word 'soldier'), and sometimes seizing power in major cities. Their methods of punishment are similar, too. The well-known fifteenth-century *condottiere*, Braccio da Montone, once smashed the heads of nineteen monks on their monastery's anvil. He also amused himself by throwing people off tall towers in Assisi; and in Spoleto, he once pushed off a bridge a messenger who had brought him bad news. For a short period, he ruled Rome, during which time the Eternal City fell into disrepair, being dominated by gangs and thieves. When he was forced out of Rome in 1422, in retribution Braccio destroyed the marble dams on the River Tiber, thus causing serious flooding in the city. Da Montone died in battle – wounded, he was deliberately left to suffocate under a horse that had fallen on him. At the insistence of Pope Benedict XIV, who hated him, he was buried in unhallowed ground.

In Russia's mind-boggling descent into the realms of the archaic in the twenty-first century, the demonstrative punishment of a deserter highlights a frightening evolution of 'instruments of education': from a champagne bottle used in the 'Dal'ny' police station in Kazan; via the sweeping brush with which they raped prisoners, as shown in Vladimir Osechkin's prison video archive released in December 2021; through the dumbbell with which the police tortured the poet Artyom Kamardin in Moscow; all the way to Prigozhin's sledgehammer.[2] What is next in this Russian horror film? A jackhammer? A chainsaw? Violence in Russia is taking on ever more sophisticated and grotesque forms; its metastases are finding their way into every organ of the social body.

It is typical that the executed prisoner in the video himself passed through various institutions of violence on his life path. He served as a conscript in the army and then as a warrant officer in the police force. After leaving the service, he was involved in the criminal underworld of the 1990s, and in 1999 he killed a person in 'some messy business' ('They could've killed me; I killed them', was how he summed it up to the Ukrainian journalist Ramina Eskhakzai), and was sentenced to twenty-four years in jail; it seems that they added on time for other unsolved crimes. He tried to escape along with three others; he was one of only two of them who survived, and a further four years were added to his sentence. He was due to be released in 2027. He was doing time in a 'red' labour camp for former law-enforcement officers, where he was considered 'a criminal authority' and was given privileges that otherwise were not allowed, such as the use of a tablet and a phone. He met his second wife through the Internet and they married in the prison church. Then, unbeknown to his family, he was recruited into Wagner, sent to the front, ran away, was captured, returned to Russia in a prisoner exchange and finally underwent the terrifying punishment.

The war has revealed and legitimized all the violence that has been the internal glue of the mechanisms of power in Russia. But now this hidden violence has broken out into the open – it has captured the state and will almost inevitably overthrow it: the government that has been pounding Ukrainian homes and power stations with its Iskander missiles and Grad shells is bound to receive in return its own sledgehammer as the principal agent of domestic politics. This ultimate loss of the state's monopoly on violence will spill over onto the streets and into the corridors of power itself – in the next few years, Russia can expect an explosion of violence the like of which has not been seen since the 1990s or even earlier periods of its history. And Yevgeny Prigozhin will be just one of the players in the rapidly growing 'market of violence', leading to the redistribution of property and power – after all, it was Lenin who taught that an unsuccessful imperialist war turns into a civil war. The era of the sledgehammer is coming to Russia; to paraphrase John Donne: 'Send not to know whom the hammer is beating, because it is beating you.'

War as a National Idea

Guns on the Wall

One of Russia's favourite sports is the search for a national idea. In the past thirty years, democracy and the market economy have tried to fill this role, as have 'joining the community of civilized nations' in the 1990s; doubling GDP in the early 2000s; building a 'sovereign democracy' and becoming an 'energy superpower' later on in the decade; annexing Crimea and bringing together 'the Russian world' in the 2010s. In 2022, the thirty-year search was ended. After wandering in the barren desert of the post-Soviet transition, Russia has finally found its ultimate national idea – and that idea is war.

This discovery is so simple and obvious that Putin should be given a special state prize or medal for it, something that he does not yet have. It is as if, once all social contradictions and elite strife were removed, Russia accepted its usual anatomical form with relief, and occupied the ecological niche that history had assigned for it. The war washes forth in a huge wave from the television screens and from the propaganda accounts on Telegram, backed up by billboards in the streets and placards at bus stops, where, instead of advertisements for deodorant, there are pictures of some dead 'heroes' of the invasion of Ukraine that no one has ever heard of. In school classrooms, children write letters to soldiers and put together parcels to send to the front, and in schools whose former pupils have died in the war, they set up 'the heroes' desks'. In the provinces (Moscow and St Petersburg have registered hardly any losses!), the notifications of deaths keep coming like in previous wars, followed by the zinc coffins with 'Cargo-200', the military term for bodies of killed soldiers.

At the funerals, the women habitually crumple their handkerchiefs while the men stand miserably off to the side, smoking, and the military commissar in his shabby shirt comes up with the usual platitudes and calls for more to come forward to fill the ranks; everything is exactly like it is in war films, history textbooks and family traditions: 'Our grandfathers fought',[1] our fathers fought, now we're going to fight. It is as if, all these years, Russia agonizingly remembered its traditional way of life and now has finally found it again. The authorities and society are once again in harmony, and someone in far-off Buryatia thanks the state with tears in their eyes for bringing home across 5,000 kilometres the body of their paratrooper nephew who was killed in Ukraine: 'Not for nothing do they say that we don't leave our boys behind!'[2]

By and large, war is the basic ontology of Russian society, the optic through which the Russian person sees life. There is the centuries-long war of a repressive state colonizing the population, whom the authorities see as an inexhaustible natural resource. And on the other hand, there is the war of the individual against the state, their attempts to deceive it and steal from it, that the Russian sociologist Yury Levada wrote about, defining his understanding of *Homo sovieticus*[3] as 'sly man'. It is a war between people in a divided, atomized and embittered society; a war in all its institutions, in the police and in prisons, in schools and in families; a patriarchal war of men against women and adults against children; a war of the centre against the periphery, and a war of the Empire against the colonies.

Russia has been marching to war throughout Putin's entire time in office, marked by grand military parades: on 9 May 2008, heavy weaponry returned to the Victory Day parade for the first time in twenty years, and three months later Russian tanks rolled into Georgia. Through the efforts of Vladimir Medinsky and his Military Historical Society, military history became the main historical genre, and the patriotic writer Zakhar Prilepin compiled a history of Russian literature called *Platoon: Officers and Militias in Russian Literature.* Militarism became the ideology of the state, war seized the imagination of the nation, Chekhov's guns[4] were hung on all the walls; yet we stubbornly refused to take all this seriously, regarding it simply as a postmodern game and political theatre.

In fact, the Kremlin has been preparing for a major war for at least fifteen years, since 2007, when Putin, in his speech at the Munich Security Conference, outlined his plans for changing the existing world order. In the same year, those in the Kremlin became absorbed by the fantasy novel by Mikhail Yuriev, *The Third Empire*, in which the author described an expansionist Russia of the future with an emperor and his personal guard at its head. (A year earlier, Vladimir Sorokin's anti-utopian novel *The Day of the Oprichnik* had been published, in which he described the Russian monarchy of the future that brought together elements of the Russia of the times of Ivan the Terrible with digital and genetic technologies.) Many of the events of subsequent years partially repeated the topics in *The Third Empire*, which led many to consider the author (who died in 2019) as a prophet and as one of the spiritual fathers of the ruling regime, along with such apocalyptic visionaries as Alexander Dugin and Alexander Prokhanov (both ultra-conservative thinkers and ideologues of the new Russian expansionism and fascism), who for decades had been calling on the Kremlin to wage a global war. Today, war has become the Kremlin's main political technology, the basis of its legitimacy ahead of the presidential elections in 2024,[5] the instrument used to mobilize the economy and to consolidate the elite and the electorate. Having killed democracy and the Constitution, Putin can now rule only with the help of a 'state of emergency', whether that is the fight against 'the colour revolutions', the annexation of Crimea, the struggle against Covid, or the war in Ukraine.

War as Identity

This war marked a radical break for Russia from the previous thirty years of the post-Soviet period, from global markets and from international institutions. It brought Russia under unprecedented sanctions and made it a global pariah – yet, surprisingly, it did not lead to social or internal political destabilization. Most of the population took it as something that was meant to happen, clothing themselves in it as if it were their grandfather's old military overcoat.

The propaganda mill worked well. As usual, the world was divided into 'us' and 'them', and the vast majority of the population developed a complex psychological defence in order to justify, accept or just ignore the war, creating a zone of comfort, a kind of shell, inside which they could live and function as they always did. The war has been normalized and absorbed into everyday life, into the daily news bulletins, and the people regard it as a state necessity, which is above any criticism in Russia, because the leadership at the top 'knows best'. The anti-war minority are scattered and silent; the policy has been adopted of squeezing dissenters out of the country, coupled with large-scale repressions of those who dare to speak out against the war (for example, local deputy Alexei Gorinov was given a seven-year jail sentence; the opposition politician Ilya Yashin, eight and a half years; and another opposition leader, Vladimir Kara-Murza, is now facing trial under a new article of the Criminal Code: 207.3, on 'discrediting the army'). These measures brought results. Anti-war protests were marginalized, stifled and, at least for the time being, incapable of shaking the sociopolitical stability.

Furthermore, it seems that the war has proved to be a rallying point where Putin's regime, the elite and the population can all come together, 'a moment of truth': a new anchor for Russian identity. Despite the shortage of imported goods and components, the rise in prices and the shutting down of production as a result of sanctions, a significant part of the population has developed a sense of national unity in standing up to external pressure. And the political and business elites feel enthusiastic amid unprecedented challenges for management. Clearly, this will not be a long-term trend, and sooner or later the worsening economic situation will lead to greater discontent; but for now, this is giving the Kremlin solid political support, legitimacy and a mandate to continue the war.

A good example was the scandalous interview given by the director of the State Hermitage Museum, Mikhail Piotrovsky. Among other stunning pronouncements, he coined a totally fascist phrase: 'On the one hand, war is blood and killing. But on the other hand, it's the people's self-affirmation, the self-affirmation of the nation.' Beginning as the Kremlin's wild fantasy, the war against Ukraine and the whole world has become the self-affirmation of the Russian political nation, and, paradoxically, by 2022 the only platform for collective self-determination in the country. The war in Ukraine is endowed with all the attributes of moral righteousness; in the mass consciousness, it is an act of retribution, righting a global injustice, the fundamental disbalance in relations between Russia and the world, the long-awaited 'answer' to the West. The war is so symbolically intensive that its very name is taboo: the word 'war' (*voina*) must not be said aloud or spelled out, under the threat of a prison sentence. It can be written only with asterisks: w*r, rather like how devout Jews write the word

'G-d'. Incidentally, Russian censorship has also forbidden the writing of the word 'peace' (*mir*), seeing it as a protest against the war, leading comedians to suggest that the title of Leo Tolstoy's novel should be written *** *and* *****.

War as an End in Itself

It does not really matter to the Kremlin that the blitzkrieg failed and that the war is not going according to plan. Russia has always fought clumsily, awkwardly, with unscrupulous means and high casualties among both its soldiers and the civilian population (as the economist Alexander Prokhorov writes in his book *The Russian Model of Management*, nearly all tasks in Russia are completed using an excess of resources). As the war proceeds, it becomes clear that its goal is no longer a swift victory and the occupation of Ukraine – but the war itself. This is what the political scientist Vladimir Pastukhov said in an interview:

> The aim of this war is – war. That part of the Russian leadership that we call 'the technocrats' has developed the concept that war is the normal state of affairs, a healthy and useful condition for Russia to be in. You have to keep a close eye on this war, like you would a low flame on the gas burner. Sometimes you prepare things on a high flame, but there are other soups that simmer away for hours on a low flame. This war for them is such, on a low flame, and they want to leave Russia on it and keep it bubbling, so that in a few years there'll be a completely different cultural soup, which is the one they need. They reckon that while they keep it simmering on a low heat Europe will burn itself up and collapse into hell.

Ukraine itself is not the target, but merely an excuse, a prelude to the permanent world war that was promised in Yuriev's book and that turns out to be the true destiny of Russia and the only hope for its own revival. The thinking goes like this: don't just patch up your leaky hut, but set fire to the whole village in order to lay claim to domination of the ashes. In fact, by 2022, Putin's Russia could suggest nothing to the outside world except war. History has come full circle, and in carrying out its retro-dream, Putin's Russia is no different from the Soviet Union in the early 1980s: a decrepit Empire, with sanctions slapped on it, barking at the outside world, mired in a hopeless colonial war, and having lost its friends and allies and the last crumbs of its reputation. Today's Russia is a zombie copy of that USSR, risen from the grave, that very 'Evil Empire', in Ronald Reagan's words, that can bring nothing to the world but war – which has become its national idea, both its purpose and its final farewell.

The Unfinished Work of 1945

The World in Search of a Bunker

Leaving Russia in the first weeks of the war in March 2022, I arrived in Lithuania and came across something that I have not seen since Soviet times: shortages – the shops had run out of salt and matches. In the next few days, I obtained some salt from a neighbour, then once again it appeared in the shops. Meanwhile, iodine disappeared from chemists' shops; it is said that, in the event of radiation, you should drink it half an hour before exposure and for two days afterwards. April in the Baltic States passed relatively peacefully, but then there were further bouts of panic ahead of 9 May, as some believed that Putin was preparing to mark Victory Day either with mobilization in Russia or by carrying out nuclear strikes on European cities. Trouble was expected in Riga (and it did occur at the memorial to Soviet soldiers, where local Russian-speakers held a demonstration in support of Russia). In Germany at the same time, in the light of the war in Ukraine, they discussed reintroducing the system of public bomb shelters that they had during the Second World War and the Cold War. A real 'bunker boom' has continued in both Europe and the USA: the demand for private bomb shelters costing from 50,000 to a million dollars has increased ten-fold.

We might grin at the paranoia of these impressionable Europeans and Americans, but it remains a fact that the war in Ukraine has raised the temperature in the world as never before for post-War generations. Neither the war in Iraq nor the wars in Yugoslavia had such a deep systemic effect. The US president, Joe Biden, blamed Russia for the forty-year high inflation in the USA: 'Putin's price spike hit here and around the world hard in May: high gas station fuel prices, energy prices and food prices accounted for about half of the monthly price increase, and gas prices rose by two dollars a gallon.' In his turn, Putin noted – not without a certain glee – that 'They're already linking my name to inflation, but this has got nothing to do with us.' Just as he said about Russian soldiers at the time of the seizure of Crimea in 2014: 'They aren't there' (*ikh tam net*).

Events that were just as dramatic unfolded in the summer of 2022 in the food markets: the world was threatened by a genuine catastrophe. Because of the war and the Russian blockade on Ukrainian grain, millions of tons of grain remained in the fields, rotted in silos or were simply stolen by Russia (at least half a billion dollars' worth), condemning tens of millions of people in Africa and Asia to starvation. As the historian Timothy Snyder reminded us, the idea of exerting control over Ukraine's grain was not new – it had equally attracted both Stalin and Hitler. The former caused the Holodomor in Ukraine in 1932–3, which led to 4 million deaths; the latter strove to reach Ukraine's grain to send it back to Germany and thus leave millions of Soviet citizens to starve. Today, Putin is using the same tactic, blackmailing the world with a grain blockade, at the same time reckoning on a flood of refugees into Europe from North Africa and the Middle East, the principal regions using Ukrainian grain. The tactic of weaponizing migrants has already been well used by his colleague Alexander Lukashenko in Belarus, where the authorities invited tens of thousands of immigrants in 2021–2, primarily from Iraqi Kurdistan, instructed them how to violate the EU border into Poland, Latvia and Lithuania, and armed them with wire-cutters and axes, provoking a migrant crisis in Europe.

The Weaponry of the Weak

From time immemorial, dealing in fear has been Russia's speciality. There is an apocryphal tale, attributed to either Emperor Nicholas the First, or Alexander the Third, that they personally inscribed in the margin of a geography textbook for cadets submitted for their approval: 'Russia is not an industrial, agricultural or commercial power; Russia is a military power, and its task is to be a threat to the whole world.' (It's more likely that it was Nicholas, who was known for meticulously delving into all the affairs of the Empire every day, from Pushkin's writings to the daily routine in military settlements.) I have been unable to locate the source of this quotation – but even if it is apocryphal, the saying reflects exactly Russia's place in the geographical and mental world map. Throughout the centuries, Russia has hung over Europe as the heir to the Asiatic hordes from the East, and it is in wars with Russia (as well as Turkey) as Europe's constitutive Other, that a European identity has emerged.

At the same time, Russia has presented the world with different aspects of itself: mystics, 'spirituality' (a particularly successful export), femininity and the 'enigmatic Russian soul'. It is no coincidence that, in many of the James Bond films, 007's antagonist is a female Russian spy – at once perfidious yet attractive. Finally, in the twentieth century, Russia demonstrated yet another unique aspect of modernization: the cultural explosion of the Russian avant-garde art, as well as the political avant-garde – the Russian Revolution produced an energy that carried the country almost through to the end of the century. For many developing countries, the Soviet modernization project presented an alternative to liberal capitalism, which was the basis of the USSR's 'soft power'.

However, by the mid-1980s, after Soviet tanks rolled into Budapest in 1956 and Prague in 1968, after the USSR invaded Afghanistan in 1979 and martial law was introduced in Poland in 1981, the Soviet alternative faded, and all that was left in this superpower's arsenal was the tried and tested load of military threats. The USSR remained large, armed and dangerous enough to threaten the West with its SS-20 missiles, to wage colonial wars and support terrorist regimes, to shoot down the Korean airliner in 1983, to poison half of Europe with radiation from Chernobyl in 1986. Modern Russia is in the same position: it is too weak to create a new world, but dangerous enough and sufficiently integrated into global networks to destroy the old world, threatening it with cataclysms, instability, new wars and a nuclear catastrophe.

In fact, Russia is engaged in the production and capitalization of threats, working on a fertile ground of fear that has been laid down historically in the West's subconscious. Such a production of fear has its own specific definition: terrorism, making an impact on the society and the institutions of power through violence and intimidation. At the level of the state, today's Russia is engaged in terrorism: military, energy, food, migration, information, chemical (remembering the poisoning of Alexander Litvinenko, the Skripals and Alexei Navalny) and, as a form of blackmail, nuclear terrorism.

As a rule, terrorism is the weapon of the weak – the Palestinians, the Islamists, the left-wingers – who are trying to crack large systems by using asymmetric ways of operating against a superior opponent, using demonstrative cruelty against random people in order to scare the government and the population. This is exactly the tactic that Putin is using now, compensating for Russia's obvious economic, technological and foreign policy weakness. He began his time in office as 'the modernization president', rather like Mahathir bin Mohamad in Malaysia, Tony Blair in Britain, and Bill Clinton in the USA, each of whom was a world leader who tried in their own way to adapt their country to globalization. Paradoxically, after twenty years, Russia has become truly globalized – but this time as a spoiler, a terrorist and the key threat to the modern world order.

Repeating 1945

Thus, Russia's place on the world map has been determined: if the West previously thought that Russia would remain on the fringes of the world system, exchanging its natural resources for consumer goods, and holding back Eurasian chaos with the help of a repressive state, then in the twenty-first century this utopia has dissipated. From a provider of raw materials, Russia has turned into a terrorist and a blackmailer. As the war in Ukraine goes on, and strategic planners try to assess where Putin will strike next – Georgia or Moldova? Poland or Lithuania? – the scale of the catastrophe is becoming more apparent. This is not simply a regional conflict on the fringes of Europe, as many Western politicians may wish to think, but the greatest challenge to the West since the Second World War.

We must not fool ourselves: even though the shells are crashing into Ukraine and people are dying there, a full-scale war is already taking place across the whole planet – probably just what was planned in the Kremlin, obsessed with absurd ideas of the inevitability of the Third World War. In this, Russia does not have superior military might (the myth about 'the world's second-best army' was shattered near Kyiv in February and March 2022), or economic potential, or significant human, technological or information resources; but it does possess one undoubted asset – fear, and the ability to influence global processes far beyond its borders. And that is even before we consider Russian nuclear weapons and the unpredictable possibility of nuclear confrontation, which will simply increase as and when it becomes clear that Russia cannot win this war by using conventional weapons.

There is no way back to the world of 2021. Humankind is in a downward spiral of confrontation, and we are already in the situation of the Third World War, whether or not we wish to call it that. This is no longer like Milosevic's invasion of Kosovo, or Saddam Hussein's attack on Kuwait; it is even less like the Cuban Missile Crisis of 1962. The closest analogy we can draw is Europe in 1938, when the talk was about not only Adolf Hitler's *Anschluss* of Austria and the annexation of the Sudetenland, but the re-drawing of the whole world order. At that time, Europe's near-sightedness and indecisiveness, and the policy of appeasement of the aggressor, led the world to catastrophe; this lesson must be learnt.

Without a radical solution to 'the Russia problem', global security cannot be guaranteed. This demands a coordination of resources by the international community not seen since the Second World War. For too long, Russia had been waving in front of itself the mystical figure of '1945' and the slogan, 'We Can Repeat It!', and the end result of that was the invasion of Ukraine. But, in fact, it is the West that should repeat 1945. At the time, the work was only half-finished: of the two bloody dictatorships that were throwing out a challenge to the liberal world order, only one was defeated. But because of this victory, another, no less dangerous, empire was strengthened. It existed through the twentieth century, partly fell apart, but has been resurrected in the twenty-first century, and once again is threatening humanity and throwing down a challenge to the free world. It is time for the West to finish the work of 1945.

Notes

Introduction

1 Marshall T. Poe, *The Russian Moment in World History*. Princeton University Press, 2003.

2 Richard Pipes, *Russia under the Old Regime*. New York: Charles Scribner's Sons, 1974.

3 Alexander Etkind, *Internal Colonization: Russia's Imperial Experience*. Cambridge: Polity, 2011.

4 Yuri Lotman, *Besedy o russkoi kul'ture. Byt I traditsii russkogo dvoryanstva (XVIII – nachalo XIX veka)*. [Talks about Russian Culture: Everyday Life and Habits of the Russian Nobility (18th – Early 19th Century)]. Moscow: AST Publishers, 2020.

5 'FSB' is the Russian abbreviation for the name of the Federal Security Service: Federal'naya Sluzhba Bezopasnosti.

6 Samuel Greene and Graeme Robertson, *Putin vs. the People: The Perilous Politics of a Divided Russia*. New Haven, CT: Yale University Press, 2019.

7 Kristina Rotkirch and Anna Ljunggrenn (eds.), *Contemporary Russian Fiction: A Short List. Russian Authors Interviewed by Kristina Rotkirch*. Chicago: Northwestern University Press, 2008.

8 Sergei Medvedev, *The Return of the Russian Leviathan*. Cambridge: Polity, 2020.

9 Michel Foucault, *The Birth of Biopolitics: Lectures at the Collège de France 1978–1979.* New York: St Martin's Press, 1979.

10 Rosgvardiya was created by President Putin in 2016, effectively as an internal army for keeping the peace within Russia's borders. It answers directly to the president. It is estimated to be some 360,000 strong. [Translator's note, hereafter '[Tr.]'.]

11 Zygmunt Bauman, *Retrotopia.* Cambridge: Polity, 2017.

12 Svetlana Boym, *The Future of Nostalgia.* New York: Basic Books, 2001.

13 Masha Gessen, 'The Russians Fleeing Putin's Wartime Crackdown', *New Yorker,* 28 March 2022: www.newyorker.com /magazine/2022/03/28/the-russians-fleeing-putins-wartime-cra ckdown.

14 Extended Meeting of the Ministry of Foreign Affairs (MFA) Collegium, 18 November 2021: http://kremlin.ru/events/preside nt/news/67123.

15 Vladislav Surkov, 'Kuda delsya khaos? Raspakovka stabilnosti' [Where Has Chaos Gone? Unpacking Instability], *Aktualnye kommentarii,* 20 November 2021: https://actualcomment.ru/ku da-delsya-khaos-raspakovka-stabilnosti-2111201336.html.

16 Timothy Snyder, 'We Should Say It: Russia Is Fascist', *New York Times,* 19 May 2022: www.nytimes.com/2022/05/19/opinion /russia-fascism-ukraine-putin.html.

17 Vladimir Pastukhov, 'Poslednyaya grazhdanskaya voina' [The Last Civil War], *Vazhnye Istorii,* 14 March 2022: https://istori es.media/opinions/2022/03/14/poslednyaya-grazhdanskaya-voi na.

18 Timofei Sergeitsev, 'Chto Rossiya dolzhna sdelat' s Ukrainoi' [What Russia Should Do to Ukraine], *RIA Novosti,* 3 April 2022; archived copy: https://archive.ph/FoMBp.

19 Mikhail Epshtein, *Proektivny slovar' gumanitarnykh nauk* [A Project Dictionary of Humanities]. Moscow: NLO Publishers, 2017, pp. 261–2.

Part I The Anatomy of Violence
The State Came after the Body

1 A video recording, with sound, was leaked to the Internet and published by the opposition newspaper *Novaya gazeta* in 2018.

2 In 2014 the Ukrainian film director Oleg Sentsov was seized in Crimea after it was annexed by Russia. He was thrown into prison accused of terrorism, and he went on hunger strike for 145 days. He was freed in 2019 in a prisoner exchange between Russia and Ukraine.

3 This was a terrorism case fabricated by the FSB in 2018. Under-age schoolchildren were thrown in prison and were tortured under interrogation.

4 FSIN is the Federal Service for Carrying Out Punishment (Federal'naya Sluzhba Ispolneniya Nakazany), the directorate in charge of prisons and corrective facilities.

5 Common types of torture in police stations and prisons are: tying prisoners' hands and feet behind their backs and hanging them on a hook from the ceiling; making them sit with the neck of a champagne bottle up their back passage; and putting a plastic bag over people's heads so that they start to suffocate.

6 www.levada.ru/2018/11/04/pytki-zaklyuchennyh.

7 OMON stands for 'Special Purpose Militia Units' (Otryad militsii osobogo naznacheniya). They were introduced towards the end of the Soviet period, when social unrest was leading to an ever increasing number of demonstrations. When the militia were renamed 'police' after the break-up of the USSR, the name OMON remained. [Tr.]

8 Official English version of the Constitution of the Russian Federation: www.constitution.ru/en/10003000-03.htm.

9 This law was passed by the Federal Assembly in December 2012 in response to the Magnitsky Act, which had been adopted by the US Congress. Under this law, Russia forbade the adoption of its orphans by foreigners, which effectively sentenced to death 265 children who had serious medical issues but who had already

found adoptive parents in the USA. Many of these children have now died.

10 In 2014, in response to Western sanctions imposed after the annexation of Crimea, Russia introduced an embargo on Western meat and dairy products and vegetables, and set about crushing forbidden products using bulldozers and burning them in mobile crematoria.

Back to 1937

1 A period between August 1937 and November 1938 when some 700,000 people were shot.

The Final Diagnosis

1 This is a play on an old Soviet joke that ran, 'We've come to an agreement with the authorities; they pretend to pay us and we pretend to work'. [Tr.]

People as 'The New Oil'

1 Cited in 'God na samoizolyatsii, Ekonomika l zanyatost' naselenia' [A Year in Self-Isolation: Economy and the Employment of the Population], *Nikitski Club* (Moscow) 112, 2021: http://nikitskycl ub.ru/wp-content/uploads/2021/03.

The Zoos of Terror

1 US Department of State, Bureau of Democracy, Human Rights and Labor, *2020 Country Reports on Human Rights Practices: Russia.* 30 March 2021: www.state.gov/reports/2020-country-re ports-on-human-rights-practices/russia.

The Generator of Entropy

1 Sergei Karaganov, 'Mirovoi shtorm I russki kurazh' [The World Storm and Russian Courage], *Russia in Global Affairs*, 28 October 2020: https://globalaffairs.ru/articles/mirovoj-shtorm-i-russkij-ku razh.

2 See Sergei Medvedev, 'In Search of Past Glory: Russia's Cultural

Statecraft in the Age of Decline', in Tuomas Forsberg and Sirke Makinen (eds.), *Russia's Cultural Statecraft*. London and New York: Routledge, 2022, pp. 226–38.

3 Ibid.
4 Iver B. Neumann, *Russia as Europe's Other*. Florence: European University Institute, 1996.
5 Boris Groys, 'Rossiya kak podsoznanie Zapada' [Russia as the Subconsciousness of the West], in *Utopia I obmen* [Utopia and Exchange]. Moscow: Znak, 1993. See also Sergei Medvedev, 'Russia as the Subconsciousness of Finland', *Security Dialogue* 30(1), 1999, pp. 95–107.

Part II The Memory Crusade
Kolyma by the Kremlin
1 One aspect of Soviet nostalgia that is promoted by Russian propaganda is the memory of Soviet *plombir* – 'the best-tasting ice cream in the world'.
2 A region in the distant far northeast of Russia, notorious for its labour camps.

Memorial to Russian Resentment
1 Vladimir Svyatoslavovich was the Great Prince of Kyiv, who oversaw the Baptism of Rus' in the year 988. In 2016 a memorial to him was erected on the Borovitsky Hill by the Kremlin gates.
2 Viktor Yerofeyev, 'Rossiya – rodina slonov i avtomata Kalashnikova' [Russia is the Birthplace of Elephants and the Kalashnikov Rifle], *Deutsche Welle*, 19 September 2017.

Thus Spake Zhirinovsky
1 'The garages': rows of boxes for the cars of people who live in the surrounding blocks of flats are typical in the suburbs of Russian towns. Being used to fixing their cars themselves, Russian men spend much of their spare time there, meaning that these garages become a kind of social club and town community. Workshops spring up and they have their own 'garage economy'.

2 This is taken from Alexander Pushkin's poem *The Song of the Prophet Oleg*, reflecting the age-old Russian dream of seizing Constantinople. [Calling the city by the Russian name of 'Tsargrad' reflects this. – Tr.]

3 Maidan Nezalezhnosti (Ukrainian for 'Independence Square') is one of the main squares in Kyiv where, first in 2004, then again in 2013–14, hundreds of thousands of protesters gathered, which led to the revolution and the change of regime.

4 Alexander Dugin is an ultra-conservative philosopher; Alexander Prokhanov, a neo-Stalinist political writer; Eduard Limonov (now deceased), a non-conformist writer who praised violence and founded the quasi-fascist National Bolshevik Party. The reference to 'Satan's ball' is to Mikhail Bulgakov's novel *The Master and Margarita*.

5 Jehovah's Witnesses are a banned sect in Russia. Most of their adherents have spent long periods in jail.

6 Ivan Ilyin (1883–1954) was a Russian philosopher, monarchist and Slavophile. When he emigrated after the 1917 Revolution, he supported fascism. It is thought that Putin was influenced by his works.

The Offering Made to the Ninth of May

1 On 17 July 1944, 60,000 German soldiers and officers were marched through the streets of Moscow, with water trucks following behind them.

2 The black and yellow ribbon started out as the ribbon of the St George Cross, a military decoration of the Russian Empire. Nowadays it has become the symbol of Russia's victory in the Second World War and the principal emblem of the new patriotism.

3 Alexander Blok, 'The Twelve'; English translation: http://secondarylaresources.weebly.com/uploads/1/0/4/7/10473434/blok_12.pdf.

A Long Farewell to Empire

1 A popular newspaper in Russia in the second half of the nineteenth century and the start of the twentieth.

2 A period in European history, between the fourth and sixth centuries, marked by the fall of the Western Roman Empire and by large-scale migrations of various tribes.

3 This is an ideological concept dreamt up by the Kremlin, calling 'the Russian world' any place where Russian-speakers live.

4 The name of the Russian-speaking lands on the left bank of the River Dnieper that harks back to the eighteenth century.

5 English translation by David Magarshack of *Myortviye Dushi* [*Dead Souls*], by Nikolai Gogol (Harmondsworth: Penguin Books, 1976), p. 83.

6 Taras Shevchenko (1814–61) was a Ukrainian poet and public figure, who laid down the foundations of the Ukrainian poetic language and literature. Stepan Bandera (1909–59) was a Ukrainian political activist of the 1930s–1950s, and one of the leaders of Ukrainian nationalism in the Second World War and in exile. He was killed by a KGB agent. *Vyshivanka* is a traditional Ukrainian embroidered shirt.

7 Traditional Russian woman's tall headdress.

8 Vladimir Sorokin, *Telluria*, trans. Max Lawton (New York Review of Books, 2022), p. 279.

Part III The War Nation

The Zombie Apocalypse

1 This is an exact translation of Putin's comment at a press conference in reply to a question about how long Russia would fight in Syria.

Revenge of the Underground Man

1 Milan Kundera, 'An Introduction to a Variation', *New York Times Book Review*, 6 January 1985: https://archive. nytimes.com/www.nytimes.com/books/98/05/17/specials/ kundera-variation.html.

2   Joseph Brodsky, 'Why Milan Kundera Is Wrong about Dostoyevsky', *New York Times Book Review*, 17 February 1985: https://movies2 .nytimes.com/books/00/09/17/specials/brodsky-kundera.html.

3   English translation by Constance Garnett of Fyodor Dostoevsky, *Notes from the Underground*, Part I, ch. 7; www.gutenberg.org/fi les/600/600-h/600-h.htm#chap07.

4   Max Scheler, *Resentiment v strukture moralei* [Resentment in the Structure of Morals]. Moscow: Nauka Publishers, 1999, p. 49.

5   Sergei Glazyev and Mikhail Delyagin are populist economists who developed ideas about autarky, the mobilization of the economy, turning away from the US dollar, and so on. The Valdai Club is an annual conference to which pro-Kremlin politicians and Western experts are invited. The Council for Foreign and Defence Policy is an expert forum set up by Sergei Karaganov to work out recommendations for the Kremlin's foreign policy.

The Z Virus

1   These are all acts of propaganda that have been staged in Russia during the war. Directors of state institutions have made their staff, students, residents in old people's homes and even prisoners line up to form the letter 'Z'.

2   One of Putin's favourite slogans is 'To raise Russia up from its knees'.

3   An article published on the website of the state information agency, RIA Novosti, in April 2022, in which Sergeytsev openly calls for the elimination of Ukraine as a nation, a culture and a state.

4   T-shirts declaring 'I'm not ashamed' were produced in the first weeks of the war in response to calls from the whole world for Russia to be ashamed and repent.

Russia Inside Out

1   The Russian army uses the following expressions: 'Cargo-200' means 'a corpse'; 'Cargo-300', someone who is wounded; 'Cargo-400', someone concussed or a prisoner, and so on. It is customary to call a corpse a '200'.

2 Balabanov became a cult figure, and his film *Cargo-200* tells the story of how, in a provincial Russian town in the mid-1980s, the body of a Russian paratrooper who has been killed in Afghanistan is thrown onto his fiancée's bed while she is kept chained to the bed by a perverted militiaman.

3 Yury Mamleyev is a modern Russian writer (1931–2015) who founded the school of 'metaphysical realism', which was marked by an interest in the afterlife and esotericism. Vladimir Sorokin (born 1955) is a Russian conceptualist writer who experiments with language and the themes of the human body, violence and the base mythologies of Russian life.

4 Jeff Hawn, 'Neraskayavshayasya armiya' [The Unrepentant Army; in Russian], *Riddle*, 22 April 2022: https://ridl.io/ru/ne-raskayavs hayasya-armiya.

5 The chief protagonist of Nikolai Gogol's story *The Overcoat*. He is a petty clerk in St Petersburg, who has his overcoat stolen in the street, and this becomes the source of his inexhaustible suffering. This story, which created sympathy for 'the little man', is one of the classic texts of Russian culture.

6 This is a paraphrase of a famous line, 'All of Russia is our orchard', from Chekhov's *Cherry Orchard*. [Tr.]

Mobilization as Russian Fate

1 English translation by V. Tchertkoff of 'Bethink Yourselves!' (*Opomnites'!*), at www.gutenberg.org/cache/epub/27189/pg27189 -images.html. [The translation is taken from *The Times*, published in 1904, hence the phrase 'the cannon's flesh' (in modern English, 'cannon fodder') and 'divers' for 'diverse' or 'various'. – Tr.]

2 Yevgeny Prigozhin is one of Putin's closest and most trusted associates, who runs the Wagner group [a private military company, even though such a concept is banned by the Russian Constitution – Tr.]. The group was named after the call-sign of one of its commanders. In the summer and autumn of 2022, they openly recruited tens of thousands of prisoners from Russian labour camps, especially murderers and rapists who were serving long

sentences, and sent them to the frontline in Ukraine. They were promised early pardons from their sentences, or, in the event of their death, compensation to be paid to their families.

3 Allegedly said to General Eisenhower when the American commented on Red Army losses in the Battle for Berlin in 1945 – although there is no proof of this, and the expression is known to have been used earlier.

4 In his book *Exit, Voice and Loyalty: Responses to Decline in Firms, Organizations, and States* (Cambridge, MA: Harvard University Press, 1970), the American economist Albert O. Hirschman describes people's behaviour when they come up against either the worsening condition of the services they need, or state management.

5 This is the syndrome of hostages who, over time, come to sympathize with their captors, and to identify their interests with the hostage-takers' goals. This condition got its name from a 1973 bank robbery incident in Stockholm, Sweden, during which the captive bank employees became sympathetic with the robbers who took them hostage.

6 Words Putin has come out with at press conferences in recent years, when he talked about the possibility of world war and a nuclear apocalypse.

7 According to the World Values Survey, carried out in 1981 by a team of sociologists under the leadership of Ronald Inglehart, it was clearly demonstrated in Russia that the values of survival always trumped the values of self-expression.

8 Stalin's famous toast at the reception in the Kremlin on 24 May 1945 was 'for the health and patience' of the Russian people, who forgave the government the sacrifices and losses of the first years of the war and, 'believed, remained patient, bided their time and hoped'.

The Age of the Sledgehammer

1 Boris Nemtsov was shot on the night of 27 February 2015 at Moskvoretsky Bridge near the Kremlin. There is evidence that

the roots of this assassination can be traced back to the leadership of Chechnya that wanted to make a deadly 'present' to Putin; however, the investigation was never completed, obstructed by the Chechen authorities, and only the perpetrators of the crime were convicted.

2 Some of the most publicized cases of police torture in Russia in the past few years: in 'Dal'ny' police precinct in the city of Kazan, police made the detainees sit down on a champagne bottle; in the video archive of prison torture released by human rights activist Vladimir Osechkin in 2021, some episodes include prison guards raping prisoners with the handle of a sweeping brush; and in September 2022 in Moscow, the policemen who raided the apartment of poet Artyom Kamardin who had been reading anti-war poetry in the streets, raped him with a dumbbell bar.

War as a National Idea

1 'Our grandfathers fought' and 'Thank you for the Victory, granddad' have been propaganda slogans in recent years.

2 'We don't leave our boys behind!' (*Svoikh nye brosayem*) is another propaganda slogan that attempts to explain that the Russian invasion was essential 'to save the Russian-speaking population'.

3 *Homo sovieticus*, 'Soviet man', is an ironic or even a pejorative term, first used by the writer Alexander Zinovyev in his book of the same name (1982). Later, this anthropological type was described by the Russian sociologist Yuri Levada (1930–2006).

4 A dramatic principle of Anton Chekhov's was that: 'If you've hung a gun on the wall in the first act, then in the final act it should fire.'

5 In 2020, Putin altered the Constitution, allowing him to be reelected in 2024, and again in 2030.

Index